REFLECTIONS OF A FISHERMAN

REFLECTIONS OF A FISHERMAN

Geoffrey A. Smith

*With eight drawings by
Judy Whittlestone
and text illustrations by the author*

SOUVENIR PRESS

ISBN 0 285 62811 9

Phototypeset in Great Britain by
Input Typesetting Ltd, London
Printed in Great Britain by
Billing & Sons Ltd, Worcester

INTRODUCTION

After hours, days, even years of waiting, the float I had watched so intently first bobbed and then disappeared beneath the murky waters of the Stanton Canal. The thrill of that moment is still as vivid in my memory as if it were yesterday, and I could take you along the bank and point without hesitation to the exact spot where I caught my first fish, although it was well over thirty years ago. That moment began a passion for fishing which is just as strong today, although my fishing is now restricted to the pursuit of river trout, sea-trout and salmon.

I could just as easily point out the weedbed on the River Derwent, in the beautiful Derbyshire hills above Matlock, where I deceived my first brown trout, and relive the heart-stopping fight which followed.

The rock in the Shepherd's Pool on the River Spey in the rugged Highlands of Scotland, where I hooked and landed my first sea-trout at five minutes to eleven one May evening, under an onlooking sky of deep royal blue, is still indelibly imprinted in my memory. I can still, when I think of that moment, hear the reel screaming as the fish set off for Kinchurdy and see the water sparkling in the twilight when the trout swirled in front of me before he lay gasping in the net and shining like a bar of silver. Nothing can surpass the first sudden bump of a salmon taking my bait in the Lodge Pool on the same river, and the twenty-minute battle which ensued. I can still feel that awesome power taking line from the reel and bending the rod almost to its limits.

I can still see that salmon lying, glistening silver and blue, on the thwart of the boat I had used to cross the river in order to fish the pool. I was so overcome with emotion that I found it impossible to continue fishing: all the co-ordination needed to cast had gone. I walked down the river trying to compose myself with the help of several cigarettes, before returning to the boat to make sure that the fish was there and the whole episode had not merely been a dream. This supreme occasion, the ultimate in fishing, was tarnished when I returned to the boat after more perambulations, and noticed blood seeping from a wound halfway along the fish's side, where the gaff had penetrated the flesh before lifting it out of the water. The wound offensively interrupted the magnificent streamlined shape of a powerful ten-pound fresh fish. I repeatedly washed and bathed that fish in the river, hoping the scar would heal and it would be restored to its former glory. It seemed such an unfitting end to a creature which filled me with nothing but admiration. I promised that salmon that I would never, whatever the circumstances, use a gaff again. I have kept my promise over the years, preferring to use a net or a tailer which prevents any damage to a fish while it is being landed and leaves the majestic salmon to lie with elegance and dignity, even in death.

Together with these never to be forgotten and never to be repeated firsts have come many other rewards that my love of fishing has brought me: the sight of a kingfisher flying low, like an orange and turquoise-blue dart; still, misty dawns on Eyebrook reservoir and the first glimpse of the sun peeping over the horizon, bringing with it the promise of a beautiful day; the magical experience of flocks of wading birds returning at dusk, wheeling, circling and intermittently revealing their white undersides as they descend to the water, performing a winged version of a ticker-tape reception to the night. The initially annoying habits of the moorhens breaking cover and paddling across the river, or of a mallard performing a broken-wing act, creating commotion on the water in an attempt to distract attention from a young brood, must be tolerated and admired in what is, after all, their own environment. The antics of the water voles are amusing, while the soaring power or the electrifying stoop of an eagle, osprey or harrier is breathtaking.

I cannot recall how many coarse fish I caught in my boyhood, or how many brown trout I have caught in subsequent years, or how many sea-trout since I began fishing for them some fifteen years ago, although I clearly remember how many salmon I have landed.

Fishing for me is not about numbers, weights or records. Of course it is satisfying to catch fish, otherwise I would not fish at all, but it is just as much about the places to which it has taken me, far away from the noise, bustle and speed of what is called progress. It is about the people I have met and the friends I have made — Syd the comedian, Arnie the ever-thoughtful, George the organiser, Wim the perfectionist and old Fred the supreme optimist. It is about the peace, solitude and tranquillity I find by the river. The birds singing, the water chattering over the rocks or gurgling through gullies, the wind rustling the grasses or blowing through the trees, are my kind of music; the animals which frequent the banks and pastures are my constant companions; and the ever-changing seasons are all I need for my visual enjoyment.

Another joy of fishing is reminiscing about seasons past during the close season. 'Why don't you write a book?' asked George, Arnie or Syd — I cannot remember who suggested it, but it was late on a winter's evening sitting by the open fire, enjoying a pint and repeating stories told many times before. 'I would certainly have plenty of material,' I said, reminding them of our trips to Ely and Boroughbridge. 'Remember twice round the island?' Syd put in, beginning to laugh as usual. 'What about Arnie getting stuck in the mud at Eyebrook?' George gleefully remembered . . . and so it went on.

Reflections of a Fisherman is a result of that chance remark. It is a recollection of how and when I began coarse fishing at an early age, how the interest developed, the transition from coarse to fly fishing and my first few years of fishing the Derwent in the Derbyshire hills.

I hope my readers will enjoy the experiences I have recorded, but above all I hope that any lad or lass reading this book will pester, persuade and strive for a rod, reel and line and find some water on which to use them; and that any mother or father with a son or daughter with the slightest interest in fishing will help and encourage them to follow this pleasant and rewarding hobby.

It must be ten years ago now when I met a young lad with his parents on the banks of the Spey. They were staying in a cottage which allowed fishing on part of my beat. I strolled up to them and passed the time of day while I watched the lad trying in vain to cast a fly.

'He's been trying for hours, and I'm no angler so I can't help him,' his father remarked.

I spent about an hour with that lad, gave him some of my fly patterns (which made his eyes sparkle) and eventually managed to get him at least to put a fly on the water.

'He still looks in difficulty,' his father said anxiously, almost willing him to do well.

'Yes, he will be,' I said. 'The rod he's using isn't really suitable.'

'Will it be worth buying him one that is?'

'It will be a good investment and I don't think you'll regret it,' I said, looking towards the lad who was still persevering, standing by the river in his green wellingtons.

The following day I saw the lad and his parents walking towards me. He was proudly but stiffly holding a rod as if the slightest breeze would break it.

'Will you try this for me?' he asked.

'Love to,' I said. 'And a lovely rod, too,' I added after a few casts.

That boy and his parents have never missed a Spring Bank Holiday in that cottage. I have met them every year and watched a lad trying to fish change into a competent fisherman and, what is more important, a very pleasant young man.

CHAPTER ONE

It all began when we moved house and went to live on the outskirts of Ilkeston, close to the Derbyshire-Nottinghamshire border and next door to dear old Mr Hendy. I am sure he was elderly, although I was only nine at the time and impressions of age are sometimes coloured by one's own tender years. Mr Hendy's shed was a treasure house of varied and exciting items collected and stored over many years. I always felt privileged to be invited in and lovingly shown individual pieces of his history, gathered together in the belief that nothing should be discarded, since it might be required by someone or for something one day. During one of those visits, he sitting on his upturned box with its seat of faded carpet and I on a white hand-painted chair, he produced a fishing rod and reel. 'I would like you to have this, my lad,' he said very quietly. I thanked him as graciously as any nine-year-old could. I cannot help remembering how the excitement of this acquisition was tempered to some extent by the tears which appeared in the old man's eyes. Was it the thought of many happy hours never to be repeated, or sadness at losing an old friend, or were they tears of happiness from the knowledge that one of his many treasures had found a new and trusting home?

Although, over the years, I have acquired numerous rods and reels of one type or another, none remains more vivid than that first combination. The rod was a three piece and all of twelve feet long, the top section greenheart which was a name to be revered in those days. The middle section was split cane as was the bottom, except for the handle which was again solid greenheart. It did not come in a rod bag with a separate compartment for each piece as new ones do, but was held together by two carefully tied pieces of string. The stand-off rings, whippings and varnish were dark with age. The brass reel fittings, too, had a hint of age, textured by green oxides and wearing thin in places. The reel was made from wood, contrasting well with the brass support which held it in place on the rod. I saw a similar rod, although it had a much more modern reel, in action on the River Derwent in the north of the county many years later.

An opportunity to use the rod did not present itself for about two years. I was considered too young at the time to go fishing — which, on reflection, was quite sensible because it meant venturing off alone — although the area had an abundance of ponds and many tantalising miles of canal bank. At the time, however, I could not see why train-spotting, with its allied sport of placing halfpennies on the track before an express was due, or invariably arriving home sooty after standing on the footbridge, looking down the funnel of the nine-thirty slow goods to Nottingham (and every one after that, for that matter), was considered reasonable while the gentle art of fishing was not. During those two years the rod was kept cleaned and the brass well polished. I assembled and dismantled it many times whilst dreaming of river, pond or canal teeming with fish, eagerly waiting to be hooked, played and landed.

The house we had moved to was a large, double-fronted place with two square bays on either side of a coloured leaded-glass front door recessed in a porch, which had a black and white patterned tile floor. It stood elevated above the very last road which circled the town to the south, and overlooked the fields in the direction of the village we had left, which was about three miles away. I suppose it was a rural setting but it was a sharp contrast to the village life I had become accustomed to for some years. The people, except for those in the immediate vicinity, were anonymous compared with the all-knowing, all-seeing and ever-helpful village folk. I missed the twice-daily ritual at milking time of the cows lazily walking through the lanes and narrow streets from the fields to the farm and back again, and the shouts from the farm hand and the excited yapping of a not too well trained dog trying to hurry the leisurely pace of the herd which was holding up the hourly bus. I could no longer smell the mowing grass being cut during the spring or hear the familiar hum of tractors pulling the often over-loaded drays of hay to the barns for storage and winter feed. The sound of the binder clicking out sheaves of corn was no longer an integral part of my life, nor the chatter of the people as they followed behind, standing the sheaves into stooks which followed lines parallel to the perimeter hedge, ever-decreasing, but still echoing the shape of the field until they reached the centre. I missed seeing plumes of dust coming from the farmyards at threshing time when the wheat was being separated from the chaff. I used to watch for hours, almost mesmerised by the huge, unprotected wheels carrying the belts which produced the numerous mechanical processes to operate the threshing machine. The 'phut, phut' of the single-cylinder Alice Chalmers tractor providing the power was monotonous and incessant. The clatter of the rods which agitated the trays and turned the drums was endless and constant, while sheaf after sheaf of corn was manually pitchforked into the hopper, pouring an endless stream of wheat into sacks from one chute and providing straw bales for bedding for the animals from another.

The garden of our house was huge and provided some consolation for the things I missed. I remember walking along the many paths and counting one hundred and five apple trees. Until I saw that garden an apple tree was something which grew in an orchard with branches growing from a central trunk. Many of these were the cordon variety, each with a single stem, no branches and growing at an angle of about sixty degrees to the ground. These contrasted well with the espalier type of tree which had long branches spaced at regular intervals up the main stem and growing horizontally along rustic framework or along the boundary walls, providing unique decorative screens.

The house on Longfield Lane and its gardens eventually proved too large, so we moved again, to a smaller house which was situated in a crescent about half a mile up and just off the lane. This move gave me the opportunity to further my interest in fishing in a much more positive way and was a welcome change from the isolation of my last home. Several boys of my own age lived nearby, many of them going to the same school. The first fishing friend I had was Gerald, the lad next door.

We were talking one day about things in general as lads of eleven or so do, such as, 'Have you had your first fag yet?' and other serious matters, when out of the blue he mentioned that fishing was quite high on his list of interests. We made hasty arrangements for our first expedition to the 'top canal'. Early next morning everything was ready. Rod still tied together with its pieces of string. Not much time — and little inclination — for breakfast. Reel and sandwiches were packed into my father's old wartime gas mask case. Makeshift perhaps, but it served me well for many years. To get to the 'top canal' meant quite a long walk, particularly on a warm, sunny morning, along many hard, dusty roads, over the same railway footbridge I used to stand on, and then up through two or three fields to the 'top canal'. The last few hundred yards seemed endless as our excitement and anticipation increased. At last we arrived on the canal bank, hot, breathless and pretty well exhausted. No time to explore: the rods must be set up so that we could begin fishing without delay. During this time not a word was spoken; there was only fervent activity. Rod sections in place and in line. Reels in position. Line threaded through the rings. Float attached to the line and finally trace and hook joined to the nylon from the reel. I felt a tremendous sense of achievement when everything was ready. Then it happened in one sentence from Gerald: 'Have you brought any bait?' I will leave you to imagine how I felt. Two years I had waited for this moment; everything was ready for the great occasion and we had forgotten the one item which we needed before casting! How stupid. How unforgivable.

There was only one thing to do. Leaving Gerald to look after the rods, I went down through the fields, over the footbridge, along the roads to home, to take from the bread bin a quarter of a loaf before heading back to the 'top canal' once more. We did not catch a fish on our first outing, or on many after that, but I can honestly say that from that day onwards my tackle is checked and rechecked, and I have never again suffered from the lack of any item, no matter how trivial.

The part of the canal where I began fishing stood high above the Erewash Valley which was at this point dominated by a vast iron and steel works. Looking down I could see the blast furnaces, coke ovens belching forth smoke and steam, and much of the attendant plant which was segmented by the necessary lifelines of road, rail and canal. To the right lay the town of Ilkeston, rising from deep in the valley to high on the hill where the shops, houses and factories created a severe and untidy horizon. On the other side of the valley, behind the 'works' and to the left of the town, I could see green fields, golden corn, woods and copses. A rocky outcrop, known locally as Stony Clouds, stood majestically above part of the golf course which climbed the hills towards the tiny village of Stanton where I used to live and from which the ironworks took its name.

The 'top canal' was never very productive in terms of fish caught — in fact it was not productive at all — but in those formative years it had its compensations in the peace and quiet, the wild and natural life it offered, although this was somewhat limited. It did, however, probably without my realising it at the time, teach me to live with myself and

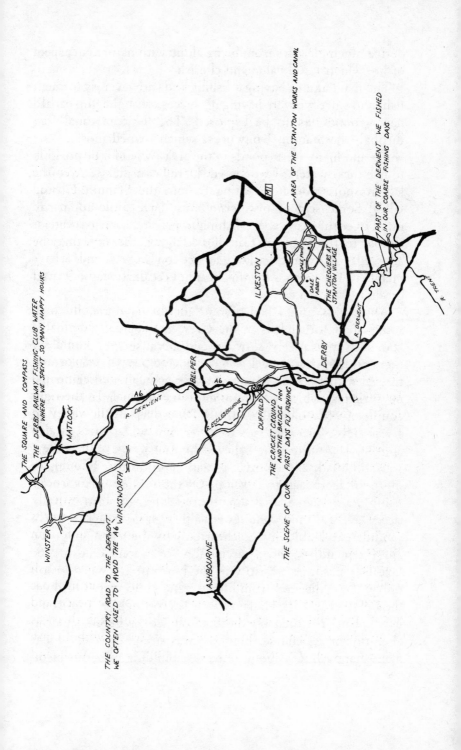

THE SQUARE AND COMPASS

THE DERBY RAILWAY FISHING CLUB WATER
WHERE WE SPENT SO MANY HAPPY HOURS

MATLOCK

WINSTER

A6

R. DERWENT

BELPER

A6

R. ECCLESBOURNE

DUFFIELD

THE COUNTRY ROAD TO THE DERWENT
WE OFTEN USED TO AVOID THE A6 WIRKSWORTH

ASHBOURNE

THE CRICKET GROUND
AND THE BRIDGE INN
FIRST DAYS FLY FISHING

THE SCENE OF OUR

DERBY

R. DERWENT

DALE POND

DALE
ABBEY

THE CHEQUERS AT
STANTON VILLAGE

ILKESTON

M1

AREA OF THE STANTON WORKS AND CANAL

PART OF THE DERWENT WE FISHED
IN OUR COARSE FISHING DAYS

R. TRENT

derive much pleasure from being alone with nature, an aspect of life which I still value and cherish.

The main aim of having a fishing rod, however, is to catch fish, and since we were having no success with the 'top canal', new ground had to be explored. The 'bottom canal' ran through the Stanton Ironworks, which owned most of the water and many other ponds in the area. Would it be possible to fish these waters? I wondered. Dare I consider it? A young lad in short trousers wanting to join the Stanton Fishing Club! Some sort of mysticism must have built up in my mind over the years about fishing in privately owned waters, almost to the point of fear of asking whether it would be allowed, or even of asking advice on how to become a member. The reasons for this I cannot recall. It was hallowed ground, I thought.

About this time I had become increasingly friendly with some of the other lads in the Crescent where I lived. This had been a relatively slow process because they had lived there all their lives and I was considered a newcomer, to be treated with a certain amount of suspicion. Gerald had made new friends, which was quite understandable since he was a couple of years older than myself. When he was thirteen and I was eleven we were lads together, but when I was twelve and he was fourteen he believed himself to be adult while I was still a lad, and so my association with other boys more my own age began to develop. Of these Mick was keen on fishing, although at that time more in thought than in practice. Dave was mildly interested, although he was not a likely candidate to be bitten wholeheartedly by the fishing bug. We all, I remember, had a fascination for water. One of our favourite pastimes was to visit the Nutbrook, a small brook only a short distance from home, which meandered through the fields from Kirk Hallam towards Nottingham until some new 'plant' required by the Stanton works necessitated an alteration in its course. Before it was straightened we spent many happy hours about its banks, building rafts out of oil

16

drums, string and logs, or swinging across the brook on a rope tied to a convenient branch. These pursuits were not always successful — unless we measured success in those days by the amount of mud and water we carried home on our clothes and the inevitable good hiding.

We began fishing in earnest when Mick begged or somehow acquired a fishing rod and its associated tackle from his grandfather. What a beauty it was, too, complete with its own cloth bag. Mind you, I would not have swopped it for mine, I thought at the time, even with its pieces of string and the fittings wearing thin. We decided to make some tentative enquiries about the fishing at Stanton. The best plan, we thought, was to visit the 'bottom canal' at the weekend, when the banks were at their busiest. Off we went down the road, chatting about fishing (mostly hypothetical, but the time passed quickly). In terms of the number of people fishing, it certainly was busy when we arrived, although a distinct atmosphere of quiet concentration and expectation prevailed, which we found a little unnerving. There was no noticeable conversation between the fishermen, even though they were only sitting a few yards apart. Every one of them had their eyes fixed on the vividly coloured floats: some red, some yellow, some black and white striped; some protruding a good two inches above the water, while others were barely visible above the water-line. As we walked along the tow-path, even the occasional crunch of the gravel under our feet seemed like thunder shattering the peace, much to our dismay. The odd eye gave us a furtive glance, almost daring us to misbehave or talk, before it returned, transfixed, to that bobbing float. Any thoughts of making enquiries about the fishing quickly faded from our minds as we warily made our way along the bank. After walking what was probably some fifty yards, but which seemed to us more like fifty miles, the line of fishermen ended for a while. There was quite a gap before a few more appeared dotted amongst and partially obscured by the reeds. We decided in that short interlude to carry on walking towards the railway which ran over the canal, and to return to the road by the track to avoid retracing our steps along the canal bank. Silence again as we approached the next fisherman.

'Interested in fishing?' he asked quite unexpectedly.

'Ye-es,' we spluttered, surprised and quite astonished at this sudden verbal address.

'A couple of lads interested in fishing here!' he shouted to his friends, leaning back on his basket and almost overbalancing in an effort to peer round the reeds.

'A good thing, too,' came the reply. Why the sudden change?

Then in the distance a whistle blew. Both men rose almost simultaneously, and one of them suggested that we should go and watch the weigh-in of the fishing match which had just finished. Now we could understand why it had been so serious in those first fifty yards. We retraced our steps and found a hubbub of noise. All those motionless figures were now moving, some in twos or threes talking, others following a rather official-looking gentleman whose duty it was to weigh and record each catch, and others whose sole aim was to relieve aching muscles by vigorous massage or an exaggerated stamping walk. Not much noise from the gravel now, I thought, as if earlier it had been deliberately noisy.

After the applause, the 'well dones', the commiserations and finally a chat with one of the officials, we wandered home well pleased with our efforts, happy in the knowledge that we only needed to write a letter enclosing a postal order and a self-addressed envelope to become Junior Members of the Stanton Fishing Club.

I awaited the post just as eagerly as at any birthday or Christmas time. Eventually it arrived, the brown-coloured envelope with a Company emblem on the front, which I hastily opened and cast aside to reveal a green booklet. Inside all the officials were listed, together with the Club rules and the waters they owned — names like Chadwicks Pond,

Roughs, Dale and 'Private', which was only to be fished by Senior Members on application for a key to its grounds. Entry forms for matches also made interesting reading and even the brightly-coloured staples which were holding the pages together had a hint of beauty. Looking at Mick's face a couple of breathless minutes later told me that his ticket had arrived by the same post.

CHAPTER TWO

To begin fishing in our new surroundings had its problems. We had homework to do in the evenings and at weekends Dave had to be considered as he had not yet aspired to the necessary tackle. Besides, there were other activities to be enjoyed, much to the annoyance of the neighbours. 'Pin and Button' provided light relief after the homework had been done — somewhat scantily I might add, particularly if the others were out first. One of us would place a pin in the woodwork over the window of a selected house, round which went a piece of cotton with a button attached to the end. One of the others, concealed behind a wall or bush, held the other end, the distance away being dependent upon the length of cotton or the degree of our bravado. As soon as the person charged with placing the pin had returned, we jerked the string and the button tapped against the window. At the slightest movement of the curtain we would stop jerking the cotton — silence. Once the curtain closed, tap, tap, tap went the button. It usually took two or three repeats of this exercise before the front door was opened, sending rays of light in our direction. At this point we disappeared at great speed, scattering into the safety of the darkness, before returning stealthily when we thought the coast was clear. Most of the neighbours, I am sure, enjoyed these encounters to some degree, and some even joined in. On more than one occasion I remember going home soaked to the skin by water descending from an upstairs window while I was placing the pin in position, which usually meant being confined to barracks for at least two nights.

When we did venture off to the canal, usually at weekends, the bait was a constant cause for concern. We watched experienced fishermen and quickly came to the conclusion that maggots were the most successful bait, while we could only manage part of a left-over loaf gleaned from the breadbin. Fishing with stale bread had its frustrations, for we had great difficulty in trying to persuade it to stay on the hook. We would delve into the centre to try and find a softer, more pliable piece to mould round the hook, but more often than not, at the flick of the rod when we were casting, the bread would fly off and land on the bank at the very instant the float and hook hit the water. Eventually we found that by slightly wetting our hands and so moistening the bread, we were marginally more successful. One drop of water too much, however, produced the same results as the dry bread. All too often, very dirty pieces of bread descended into the water from our grubby little paws, but we worked on the theory that if the water cleaned us it would also clean the bread. We persevered fruitlessly for weeks, but we were quite happy to be down by the canal, out of town, away from people and in the countryside. Only the distant sounds of the trains pulling their trucks heavily laden with iron ore, limestone or coal, were a constant reminder of how close we were to industry. Even the muted rumble of machinery blended well with the lapping of the water on the banks, the songs and calls from the birds or the rustling of the reeds and bulrushes bending and swaying in the welcome breeze.

The other waters owned by the Club were close by, so we explored. We spent some time birdnesting in the hawthorn hedgerows and in the woods surrounding the ponds. They were happy hours, despite the frustrations and lack of achievement. Success, by our reckoning, meant the acquisition of some maggots, so we made a trip to town, armed with an empty cocoa tin with some air holes pierced in the lid, to the Barber's and Sports shop. This was a combined organisation, the two areas being separated by a curtained

The Stanton Canal.

doorway. I could hear the snip of scissors percolating through the curtain, which sent shivers down my spine. Having a hair-cut — short back and sides, with a fringe at the front in the classic choirboy style — was not very high on my list of priorities at any time. How long must we wait? Time was scarce, or so it seemed, and we were impatient. Eventually the snipping stopped, followed by a 'Thank you, that's fine', an exchange of coins, brief farewells, and we were being served with maggots. A half-pint tankard of sawdust and maggots, in what proportions we could not see, was being transferred from a bin to our cocoa tin by the barber of just a few minutes ago. Clutching our tin we hurried home, pausing every now and again to peep inside to make sure all was well. We could see a seething mass of sawdust and wrigglies, which to us was a wonderful sight. After collecting our tackle, food and drink, we arrived once again at the canal, this time to compete on more favourable terms. It was sheer delight fishing with a maggot. Once held by the barb, we could cast it into the water with gay abandon, never to be lost unless it was caught on some offending piece of hedgerow.

The next hour or so passed very quickly, speeded by our increased anticipation and expectation. There was no time to explore today: full concentration on the float was required. There it was, with its red tip about half an inch above the water, occasionally tilting in the breeze or bobbing daintily in time with the ripple. Then it bobbed and almost disappeared before returning to its original position. That was not the wind *or* a ripple — or was it? I asked myself a few moments later, when it did not happen again. I could still feel the rod trembling in my hand when the float disappeared completely. A quick lift of the rod and the fish was hooked. I could actually sense and feel something moving on the other end of the line. Peace was shattered as I shouted excitedly to Mick. He came running along the bank shouting in reply. How he expected me to know the size and type of fish while it was still fighting in the depths of the water I could not imagine. Dave, who had accompanied us as an observer, appeared from somewhere, together with other anglers believing that all the commotion must mean a specimen fish or a least a fish worthy of note. When I landed my catch it turned out to be a gudgeon which must have weighed all of three ounces, give or take a gram or two; the humblest of fish, but at the time it was as exciting and exhilarating as catching a ten-pound salmon. I found it difficult to remove the hook from the lively, slippery little creature, but I tried to appear as nonchalant as I could under the circumstances, to give the impression that it had happened many times before. Dave and Mick knew the truth and so, I am sure, did the others as they returned to their respective stretches of bank. More fish followed. Mick had his first and several more after that, and so did an excited Dave when we left him in charge of one of the rods.

The following Saturday we decided to visit Dale Pond, which was about three miles away across the fields. A beautiful spot, situated roughly midway between the villages of Dale Abbey and Stanton-by-Dale, with a farm and a small row of white-painted cottages close by. It was difficult, looking at it with its mature trees and banks, to imagine that underneath the waters lay the remains of the original Stanton Works. I suppose the triumphs of the previous week had given us the incentive to set off on a walk of at least half an hour. Dave was quite useful on these occasions, acting as pack horse for some of the equipment. Another spur for our trip to Dale was that by reputation it was a good pond for bream, a fish which apparently preferred bread to the maggot, and we were back to bread again. The previous Saturday we had had our cocoa tin full of those lovely maggots, but what I did not realise was that they did not stay like that for ever. They had been in the shed for a week and when I opened the lid for a quick inspection, just before calling for Mick, I was immediately mobbed by hundreds of escaping bluebottles. They were everywhere, buzzing in excitement and flying round crazily, intoxicated by their new-found freedom. I could not persuade them to leave, not even by swinging a brush wildly in the hope of convincing them that the shed was not a safe place to be. Mick would be waiting, so I shut the door and walked away, hoping that they would disappear somewhere or somehow before anyone else went in.

We found that the walking time to Dale was much longer than we had originally anticipated. The route took us along part of the canal which we had fished many times before and past a pond called Roughs, both of which looked extremely inviting. We began to wonder if we would be better off here, but after much deliberation we decided to carry on. More stops were required for liquid refreshment, so our calculated thirty minutes actually extended to a more realistic hour and a half. I was reminded many times of the bluebottles as we walked through the fields disturbing the flies which had settled on the numerous cowpats. Arriving at Dale more than justified our decision. It looked particularly attractive in its picturesque setting. On one side wooded hills rose above the pond, giving way to the prickly gorse which grew in the fields, providing a safe haven for chirping linnets and a colourful surrounding to the pond. Beyond, fields descended into the valley before rising up to the horizon and the well-preserved and well-known landmark of the Cat and Fiddle Windmill. In the distance I could just see the trees on the hillside where the legendary hermit's cave, hewn from the sandstone, nestles high above the village of Dale Abbey, a tiny village which is dwarfed by a great east window standing isolated and naked now, but giving the visitor a visible monument to a once majestic building and a grim reminder of a troubled past.

It was only when I heard the sound of Mick's reel that my thoughts returned to the pond, and I quickly made some efforts to join him. We began to catch one or two fish which were indeed small bream. This kept us interested until the sun was directly overhead, which had the effect of making both fish and fishermen somewhat lethargic. Even the cows moved lazily and the tractors working the fields seemed to have lost their usual sense of urgency. The early evening gave us more sport until it was time to embark on the long walk home, accompanied by lengthening shadows, but even that was pleasant as we chatted about the events of the day. The nearer we were to home the more my thoughts returned to those wretched flies. Several times, as I walked down the path to the shed, I thought I heard buzzing. I opened the shed door gingerly and, to my amazement, not a single bluebottle. They must have had enough sport from me during the morning, I thought, as I carefully placed the tackle in its corner. The change from maggot to bluebottle happened many times after that, but I always put an ear to the tin and, at the slightest hint of a buzz, would take it ceremoniously to the bottom of the garden where the flies were released amongst the apple trees.

After our first trip to Dale we decided unanimously that, given the opportunity, that was the place to be, despite the inconvenience of the extra distance involved. I well remember one Sunday afternoon when Dave was out somewhere with his parents, leaving Mick and me together. We were just setting off after a hurried early lunch when Dave arrived. I distinctly remember him convincing his parents that a change of clothes was not necessary as he would not be fishing. The sport was not particularly interesting on that occasion. We tried the shallow side and the weeded side, before arriving at the wooded side which was dominated by one large tree on the very edge of the water. Nothing doing anywhere. We suddenly noticed that a rope had been tied to one of the branches high up in the tree. We had to peer round the trunk to see the other end which was attached to the tree by a nail. It hung vertically down the trunk on the water side, well concealed if one only gave a cursory glance. Once Mick released the rope from its nail we realised that it made a perfect swing, bringing back memories of days on the Nutbrook. You could just imagine it, a run down the bank, take off out over the water and back to the bank. We inspected the rope and then tested it with several tugs by the three of us before finally declaring it safe.

I cannot quite remember how we decided who should have first swing, but the honour fell to Dave. After he had made one or two trial runs down the bank to get the general feel of things, he tentatively launched himself out over the water. He failed to reach the bank the first time, but it took several more swings before Mick and I realised to our horror that he was not going to make it at all. The look on poor Dave's face and the frantic kicking of his legs suggested to us that he had grasped the gravity of the situation much more quickly than we had. It was an agonisingly long time before he came to rest, suspended over the water. We tried desperately to reach him. Even the fishing rods, held out at arm's length, were about two feet short. As he lowered himself down the rope and into the water, we saw his shoes slowly disappear, leaving rings of bubbles on the surface of the pond. There were gasps from Dave as more delicate parts of his body became somewhat chilled. He finally touched the bottom of the pond with the water at chest height. It was a relatively short distance to the bank, but the slipperiness of the silt bed gave him problems. Eventually he was close enough for us to haul him out. What a pitiful sight he made standing in a pool of water which had dripped from his clothes. His immediate reaction was to declare that he had no alternative but to leave home, but he soon dismissed that idea after we had convinced him that he did not look as bad as he feared and that his clothes would soon dry in the sun if we spread them out on the bushes, which in fact they did. His appearance when he emerged from his dressing-room amongst the trees was not quite the same as the one he had presented earlier, and the smell was not too pleasant either. His socks had a rather tight look about them, water oozed from his shoes where the uppers met the soles and his trousers no longer had a fine crease. We did not see Dave for a week after that, but as on so many similar occasion, anger and threats quickly faded and he soon returned to what we considered a normal life.

CHAPTER THREE

The summer holidays always provided plenty of time for fishing, as well as numerous games of cricket played with a bat which was heavy with age and held together with black adhesive tape. The ball, too, had seen better days, its leather being soft, out of shape and the stitching broken in places revealing its cotton and cork interior. Never the less, many centuries were scored on that field which was far from flat, and neither Australia nor the West Indies ever won a match.

When our enthusiasm for cricket faded temporarily, or the ball split completely, out came the rods and off we went fishing. Our destination was entirely dependent on our mood. Sometimes we chose the relatively short walk to the canal or Roughs, but if we felt energetic we made the effort to walk to Dale. I am sure that, but for the distance involved, we would have fished Dale more often, if not every time.

The fishermen we met were very friendly and we were given plenty of advice by other members on how and where to fish, which we accepted eagerly, and I have no doubt we learned many things about types of floats, size of hook, where to put the shot and what breaking strain line to use. As to where to fish left me in some doubt. It always seemed strange for a fisherman to be fishing in one place and at the same time telling us there were plenty of fish to be caught only five minutes away.

One fellow, while we were fishing at Dale one hot afternoon, really whetted our appetite for big fish. 'Have you come for the big bream?' he enquired, and then proceeded to show us where they were, obviously keen to impress us with his superior knowledge. He led us to a bank which looked down on some lily pads growing in that part of the pond.

'Just look at those,' he said, 'some real beauties, several are well over five pounds.'

We were amazed to see large black shapes, almost motionless, lying just beneath the surface, basking in the heat of the day and moving occasionally to expose a large dorsal fin above the surface of the water. 'Mind you, the only way to catch those is first thing in the morning, and then only by the big tree where the lily pads end and the clear water begins,' he informed us. He took us round to point out the exact spot and even told us the precise depth at which to fish before returning to his rod and basket which he had so readily left. During the afternoon we returned many times to look down in amazement and almost disbelief at those enormous fish.

The only way to be at the pond early enough to catch those fish was to camp there overnight. Mick and I often slept out at night during the summer holidays in a small two-man tent given to us by Gerald, although we did not venture any further than Mick's back lawn. We found this an ideal base for scrumping expeditions and spent much of the night prowling round the gardens in commando style and then talking and eating rather than sleeping. Another pastime which we refined into something of an art on those occasions was a competition to develop and pass as much wind as possible. We eventually measured our prowess by numerical ability because the length of time or the pungency was always open to argument. Mick always won these competitions, the decisive factor I am sure being due to his weakness for spring onions. I well remember a neighbour asking us how we had enjoyed our night out and, much to our embarrassment, enquiring about the significance of twelve-ten at one o'clock in the morning.

To us, camping overnight at Dale would merely be an

extension of our activities, the only difference being the distance from home and the extra requirements of food, drink, warm clothes and blankets. Dave was not particularly interested in this venture so he did not mind being left behind. Mick and I, having sought permission, excitedly made the necessary arrangements and repeatedly checked our modest but carefully considered inventory. As we left one afternoon, anyone would have been forgiven if they had thought we were going to join the Foreign Legion. Nearly all the Crescent came out to wave us off as we marched down the road fairly well loaded, with a saucepan for the baked beans swinging from Mick's bag to keep us in step.

Our excitement at the prospect of camping away from the confines of Mick's lawn and the prospect of early morning fishing made the journey seem quite short, despite the extra weight and no Dave to help us. We were amazed at how effortless it was to walk the three miles when absorbed in conversation about landing a huge fish and our slight apprehensions about the safari lifestyle which would make that possible. It was quite an experience choosing a site and setting up camp. The area we selected was in the open part of the field close to the pond, with a view of the farm and the cottages, which I suppose was reassuring for two young lads camping away from home for the first time. We pitched the tent and set up the rods and methodically laid out incidental pieces of equipment such as float boxes, keep nets and bait tins. It was a most satisfying sight as we surveyed the scene from the opposite bank, whilst collecting wood for the fire which would be required later in order to make a hot drink. Our mental image of a camp fire flickering in the darkness and the thought of preparing supper and eventually retiring to our small tent made fishing during the evening seem rather insignificant.

How strange, I thought, as I sat there, only half interested in the float some distance away in the water, how time normally flies during an evening's fishing; on this occasion

Dale Pond.

it seemed to take the sun an exceptionally long time before it began to descend towards the horizon, changing from its daytime yellow to the fiery orange of late evening.

At last it was time to prepare for our night under canvas. Mick lit the fire, leaving me to check the rods before placing them conveniently nearby, ready for the morning. We laid out blankets in the tent to give the impression of two beds. Then we had to boil some water for the eggs which were on the menu for supper. A wonderful picture began to emerge as the softer tones of twilight and shadows of the evening crept across the fields and the quiet of a summer night became complete. The flames of the fire flickered much more brightly now, illuminating our immediate surroundings and the cosy interior of the tent. The only sounds came from the sticks as they crackled on the fire, the water as it began to boil and the occasional moorhen clucking in the reeds, probably in disgust at our sudden intrusion. The nearly hard-boiled eggs, which we held in handkerchiefs serving as makeshift eggcups, tasted quite beautiful and the coffee afterwards seemed the

MOORHEN

best we had ever drunk, despite the slight flavour of orange juice from our earlier refreshment. After what could only be described as an apology for a wash in the pond and a brief chat by the side of the warm, friendly fire, we decided it was time to retire.

As we wrapped ourselves in the blankets we repeatedly told ourselves how comfortable it was, despite the lack of room and the unevenness of the hard, unyielding ground. Mick had quickly gone into a commanding lead in our competition, even without the aid of spring onions, when suddenly we heard noises outside the tent. Closer and closer they came, at a constant, slow, persistent pace. When we could speak again, which was some time after our initial alarm, we decided, without daring to peer outside, that it was probably the cows using that part of the field to graze. After what seemed to us like an eternity, our tent was completely surrounded by swishing noises which sounded eerie and ghostly in the still of the night. I was petrified, and a glance at Mick was not exactly reassuring: his face was almost white, even though it was lit by the orange firelight filtering through the canvas. The flickering flames reflected light from the numerous beads of perspiration which had gathered on his brow. Then suddenly the noises were punctuated with the sound of helpless laughter from Dave and his father and two more lads from the Crescent. They had decided to make sure we were settled for the night, at the same time extracting some amusement from the situation at our expense. As well as the branches which they had brought with them to swish through the grass, so creating those eerie sounds, they produced flasks of hot coffee which we all drank sitting round the dying embers of the dwindling fire, occasionally laughing hysterically at the thought of the fright they had given Mick and me. As we settled into our tent once more, we made no effort to continue the competition begun earlier, I suspect for fear of disastrous consequences.

We were up bright and early the next morning to begin

34

our quest for those monstrous bream. That was our main preoccupation, but as we walked towards the tree I could not help admiring the sights and sounds of the early morning. Mist lay in wispy strands over the fields in the valley; the call of the birds heralding the dawn was sharp and clear and the air smelt clean and fresh.

The closer we drew to the bank, the slower and lighter our steps became. We had decided earlier, during one of our numerous discussions on our plan of campaign, that Mick was going to fish first as the area between the lily pads and the tree could only accommodate one person. Stealthily he crept down to the water's edge, half crouching and with a noticeable stoop in an effort to minimise the size of his silhouette against the skyline. I remained some distance away, but still maintaining a good view of the proceedings from my position above the pond, hidden by the gorse bushes which provided a very useful screen. Mick cast with a deft flick of the wrist. I could see the float arc out over the pond before it landed on the surface with a 'plop' which echoed in the early quiet of the summer morning. The ripples radiating from the float seemed magnified in that light before they dispersed and the pond returned to the appearance of a sheet of polished glass. We had been watching the red-tipped float for about five minutes when it began to move across the water, resembling a red fin before it disappeared under the surface. With a lift of the rod Mick struck.

'Have you got him?' I asked excitedly, leaping to my feet.

'Yes!' Mick just managed before he was hanging on for dear life with his quarry heading for the other bank at alarming speed, leaving a wake from the taut line as it cut through the water. Then the fish turned, first left and then right, before darting back towards Mick who was almost in control up to that point. He could not retrieve line quickly enough and lost contact with the fish for a while. When he did make contact again the fish had made its way into the lily pads and safety, the line breaking as Mick fought both fish and submerged aquatic vegetation.

Nothing was said as Mick staggered dejectedly from his position by the pond. The whole experience rendered us speechless as we gazed at the now quiet and tranquil water. Mick found it impossible to do anything for a while; his limbs were trembling with excitement. I left him on the bank desperately trying to replace line and hook with fingers which would not respond, to try my luck in the same place. The thought of an encounter with a huge fish as witnessed from my vantage point on the bank made my pulse race and heart pound. As time went by, with the float remaining motionless in the water, we began to realise that our chance had gone, and pangs of hunger and thirst overcame any desire to carry on fishing for those large bream.

We were soon back at the tent, warming the baked beans on the open log fire in a saucepan blackened with smoke from the previous evening's unaccustomed treatment. Mick and I were happy, contented and proud when we reflected on what we had achieved and the experience we had gained in the hours after leaving the Crescent the previous day, even though our initial reason for being there at all had not been fulfilled.

CHAPTER FOUR

Mick, Dave and I pursued our interest in fishing until we reached the age of about fifteen when our circumstances and inclinations changed. I joined the Stanton Village Cricket Club and a local football team, so much of my time was spent following those activities. Cricket during the summer months was particularly time-consuming since it meant net practice every Monday and Friday evening, and a game for the school eleven on Saturday morning followed by a mad dash to the venue for the afternoon's game with the village side. More often than not, I had to take a hurried lunch in the form of sandwiches, usually on a bus, because time was often short when I eventually reached the ground.

During the years that followed I had to study for 'O' and 'A' levels, so that my time for fishing was reluctantly given up, although my interest never faded. I was still curious to see who or how many were fishing the canals or ponds and would stop and watch if the opportunity arose.

One of the cricketers from the village worked on his father's farm. We became close friends and it gave me the opportunity to work on the farm during the holidays, which not only brought me a source of income but also gave me the freedom of being out and about in the fields — on reflection a fair compensation for the lack of communication with nature which fishing had formerly provided. Dale Pond was on his land and I often looked longingly and nostalgically at its waters as I passed by on the tractor, or when I walked that way to fetch the cows up for milking.

Not all my pleasures were derived from outdoor activities,

however. A game of cricket never ended when one team had won or the match was drawn, or when rain finished play for the day, but was usually continued in some convenient hostelry. I have never worked out whether the cricket grounds were laid near to a public house or whether the breweries in their infinite wisdom built the pubs close to the cricket grounds; whichever it was, the convenience of one to another must leave our modern planners rather envious.

The atmosphere in the local after the game was quite unique. I saw enemies on the field suddenly become the best of friends and completely inseparable after four or five pints. They replayed the match several times and even changed the result with 'If only Pete had held that catch', or 'If only the umpire had not given Wilf out caught off his pad instead of his bat'. Players who had achieved success with the bat or ball rejoiced, while players who had failed drowned their sorrows; either way the outcome was happiness, good humour and a kindred spirit.

Most of the Stanton cricketers used to frequent an inn in the village called the Chequers, which was unofficially our clubhouse. Much of the Club's business took place there, on tables with decorative cast iron legs, close to an open fire with the tick of the grandfather clock in the corner, its time always showing ten minutes fast in an effort to ensure that the last drinkers were out on time. At the end of the season I replaced Monday and Friday net practice with evenings in the Chequers playing dominoes or cribbage, while discussing recent matches or reliving seasons almost forgotten with past players and locals. Some of the stories they told were long before my time and many I had already heard several times, but it was a pleasure to share in their past activities and show the same interest as they showed in our present exploits; a powerful bond was forged within the community.

All this came to an end when I left the area for three years' study at college, only returning for the odd weekend or for the longer vacations. During these three years many things changed. People at the Cricket Club changed, older members retiring from playing and new ones arriving. People at the Chequers changed. Old stagers from the village passed away and strangers took their place, although I was pleased to find that dominoes and cribbage still continued, when I called for a pint on a Monday and Friday during these vacations.

It was when I returned to the area after completing my college course that fishing again began to play an important part in my life. It happened quite by accident. I had been to see Richard, the farmer's son. Since the farmhouse was close to Dale Pond, my walk home was along the very paths and through the very fields which were so familiar from earlier years. It took me past Roughs Pond where I stopped to reflect on the times in my youth that I had spent fishing there. Suddenly I thought I recognised one of the fishermen sitting on his basket on the opposite bank, although I could not be sure as appearances change somewhat when dressed in fishing gear. As I approached the contented figure enjoying a pipe of tobacco in the sunshine, I recognised the face of one of the Stanton cricketers. Arnie was as surprised to see me as I him. As well as playing cricket for the village he also played dominoes and cribbage on our regular Monday and Friday nights at the Chequers, and although I had known him for many years he had never mentioned that fishing was one of his hobbies.

The consequence of this chance meeting was that fishing entered into the conversation more and more on Monday and Friday. George, Arnie's next-door neighbour and a frequent visitor to the Chequers, had also fished, even to the extent of taking part in matches, so it automatically followed that our enthusiasm for the sport was quickly revived and we began to make arrangements to take up our fishing activities again. We decided to fish the River Derwent, very close to where it joined the Trent in Nottinghamshire, at the end of its journey from high in the north Derbyshire hills. Although this area was new to me, George and Arnie obviously knew it well from the way they affectionately described it. We could obtain day tickets from a house near the river and conveniently *en route*, and it soon became a ritual for the three of us to fish the Derwent every Sunday morning from the crack of dawn. About this time a fellow named Dennis moved into the village, who was slowly accepted into our closely knit group, largely due to the fact that he knew George through work. The four of us soon became very close friends, although initially Dennis's outdoor sporting activities were restricted to golf. He eventually bought some fishing tackle and would join us on a Sunday morning when his golfing commitments allowed.

The recollections of one Sunday morning are still vivid in my memory. It was at a time of quite severe restrictions on access to fields due to an outbreak of foot and mouth disease in the area. We had acquired our tickets on the Saturday to save time the following morning, so we assumed it was quite in order to fish that part of the river. In spite of a thick fog I called for Dennis and then George who, surprisingly, was without Arnie that morning, and with difficulty drove down to the river where the fog made visibility almost non-existent. We parked, found the stile which gave access to the fields and proceeded to the bank. It was a cold, damp morning, which prompted Dennis to add more clothes in the form of a massive wool-lined flying suit. Dennis was a big fellow at the best of times, tall, with huge shoulders; now, having donned his flying suit, he appeared enormous and looked an alarming sight as he stood there shrouded in the swirling fog.

I began fishing at the point where we had reached the river. Dennis disappeared downstream and George decided to take up a position upstream from me and, although they were close by and within talking distance, visual contact was quite impossible. After a while I could hear George in conversation with someone. Curiosity compelled me to find out who else could be about on such a miserable morning. It turned out to be the River Bailiff who had seen the car parked in the gateway to the field and had come to inform us that the river had been closed because of the foot and mouth restrictions. He checked our fishing tickets while we apologised for being there and protested our innocence. Just as he was checking our rod licences, which are necessary in all River Authority waters, Dennis loomed up out of the fog. He resembled a big brown grizzly bear and the look of horror on the Bailiff's face told us that he had some doubt as to whether what was approaching was altogether human. With trembling fingers he inspected our rod licences and then tentatively asked Dennis for his. He told the Bailiff that he did not have one but would purchase one, as if the Bailiff handed them out like bus tickets, completely unaware that they had to be bought on a yearly basis from a tackle dealer. Under normal circumstances a fisherman without a rod licence would be reported to the Water Authority and subsequently fined, but on this occasion Dennis was only warned, I am sure because the Bailiff was relieved to see that he was in fact human and quite tame beneath that awe-inspiring exterior.

When we climbed over the stile on our return to the car the fog had lifted slightly, revealing the sign which had been nailed to the gate forbidding access due to foot and mouth disease; but in all honesty it was not visible when we entered the field an hour or so earlier.

It was a pleasure to be back fishing after so many years and a new experience for me fishing a river rather than the still waters of pond or canal. I had to learn new techniques to compensate for the erratic flow of the moving river, many of which I gained from Arnie and George. Although we enjoyed the reflective and peaceful environment, our skills and abilities were sharpened by a competition we began for the most fish caught, the prize inevitably being a pint at the Chequers the following evening.

CHAPTER FIVE

Another regular at the Chequers, who shared our fishing conversations, was a fellow called Syd, whom we believed to be one of the sports elite. The thought of fishing for trout and salmon never crossed our minds at the time, but Syd often referred to rivers such as the Hampshire Test and its salmon fishing. Syd was a representative for a firm which dealt with fire-fighting appliances, and he travelled around the country with equipment both for demonstrating to prospective customers and for fishing if the opportunity arose, which I am sure it did many times. On one occasion he mentioned the merits of fishing the river Ouse in Cambridgeshire and how he and two other representatives of the firm had spent several days on a fishing holiday there in his coarse fishing days.

Arnie, George, Dennis and I thought this an excellent idea. We asked Syd for directions and it was not long before we had planned a two-day fishing excursion. 'Planned' was not the word, really, as very little planning actually took place: we simply decided to go. We knew roughly the area and Syd did mention some hotel where he had stayed, but we did not book in advance. 'Playing it by ear' was the expression used, I recall. Our main concern was the fishing tackle. We would require plenty of hooks, groundbait and maggots. We decided to call on the morning of our departure at Tom Watson's, a well-known tackle dealer in Nottingham. Everything we needed we purchased there, including eight pints of maggots, which we placed in one large biscuit tin. It was very different, I reflected, from the odd half-pint bought years ago when pocket money would allow.

We followed Syd's instructions until we arrived at a place called Southery, where the Great Ouse meets the Little Ouse and where the hotel he had mentioned was situated. No accommodation was available and, rather than search any further, wasting valuable fishing time, we decided to look again later. We travelled to the next town, found a fishing tackle shop, bought the necessary tickets and licences, and made our way to the river where we hastily removed the tackle from the boot and began to set it up. We had travelled down in my car, which was a Corsair 2000, the executive type with plush carpets which even extended into the boot. George's shouts when he went for the maggot tin, the only item left in the boot, told us that something was wrong. Four pairs of eyes looked in disbelief at hundreds of maggots making themselves comfortable in the carpet or wriggling off in all directions. They were everywhere! Under the carpet, in the well which housed the spare wheel, round behind the petrol pipe and in amongst the jacking tools. It must have taken us a good twenty minutes to clear the boot. Every time we thought all had been retrieved another one appeared. Eventually all were collected and replaced in the tin, after we had made some minor repairs to the split in the seam. We began to fill our personal bait boxes from the communal tin, with the exception of Dennis. George, Arnie and I had acquired these boxes which had air holes in the lid and were made of plastic, ensuring a longer life than that of my cocoa tin, which had been prone to rust. Dennis, who did not fish so much or so seriously as we did, did not possess such a luxury, so we found an empty matchbox and gave him about ten maggots and told him to look after them. He must have taken this very seriously because, some two hours later, when we all met for a chat and general report on proceedings, he still had six left! We three had been tossing them into the river in great quantities to try to attract the fish, while poor

Dennis had used, on average, only one every half-hour. We immediately bestowed on him an honorary membership of the 'Maggot Preservation Society'.

During this interlude it suddenly occurred to us that the only food and drink we had between us was a packet of biscuits and a flask of coffee thoughtfully brought by George. These he duly shared out and we returned to the rods. Throughout the afternoon and evening we did not catch a single fish. We did, however, notice a fisherman on the opposite bank enjoying excellent sport. He was catching large fish at regular intervals while we did not have so much as a bite. After a while I noticed that he was using bread for his bait. How ironic, I thought, remembering my early years, when to fish with maggots was the key to success; now we had eight pints of them and not a piece of bread between us.

It must have been about eight o'clock in the evening when we decided it might be prudent to look for somewhere to stay. We had also begun to feel somewhat hungry since all that had kept body and soul together from about six in the morning was half a dozen digestive biscuits and a cup of luke-warm coffee.

After making enquiries at the first village we came to on our way from the river, we made for the Cathedral Hotel at Ely. We were assured that it was our last chance of accommodation in the vicinity as it was so late in the evening. We managed to acquire two twin-bedded rooms to save on expense, which left me sharing with George and Dennis and Arnie in an adjoining room. Just before we arrived at the hotel we passed a likely-looking eating place called the Cathedral Grill. By this time hunger had over-ridden any desire to change, so it was a quick wash and we were off. At the Cathedral Grill we were greeted by a very polite, evening-suited gentleman. 'A table for four, please,' he said to a waiter, who escorted us through to the dining-room and the table which had been allocated to us. As a matter of courtesy, he pulled each chair from beneath the table and

44

dusted it before we sat down. It was that sort of place, and although our fishing clothes were as respectable as any fishing clothes could be, we must have looked an odd quartet amongst the suits, dinner jackets and bow ties. The atmosphere was a little starchy, everyone speaking in whispers as if they were discussing top-secret information. The waitress arrived and, since we were now ravenous, we ordered a mixed grill. She was just turning to leave when Dennis called in a voice which could be heard by all: 'Can I have two chops with my grill, please, and what are you doing later, luv?' The whole atmosphere changed after the initial shocked silence. People began to talk quite freely and laugh among themselves, and I am convinced that we all enjoyed the meal much more after that chance remark had broken some of the ice.

We decided to spend what was left of the evening in the lounge of the hotel, having a pint and a game of cards, until a flock of men dressed in purple descended upon us. The Cathedral Hotel must have been holding a congress for clergymen, the majority of whom appeared to be staying in the hotel. Cards and beer did not blend too well with the orange juice and ecclesiastical conversation, or with the odd gin and tonic preferred by what appeared to be the more senior clergy, so we decided to retire.

The following morning the first person I met on my way to the bathroom was Arnie, looking absolutely ghastly. Apparently he had not slept at all the previous night, for Dennis, who had joined us straight from the night shift the morning before, had begun snoring as soon as his head touched the pillow.

'Come and listen to this,' Arnie said. The noise when he opened the bedroom door was quite frightful. 'Eight o'clock in the morning and he's still at it,' he complained, and went on to tell me that he had heard every chime from the Cathedral clock during the night and every lorry that drove along the road outside his window. It was a slight exaggeration on Arnie's part to say that the light had been swinging from its flex, but listening to the awful din, I would have believed anything possible. George, who had arrived from next door full of the joys of spring at the prospect of another day's fishing, could not contain himself when he heard the thunderous noise and Arnie's account of his terrible night. He wandered back to our room with tears streaming down his face, muttering, 'Oh dear, oh dear,' between fits of hysterical laughter.

We were all in the dining-room waiting for breakfast when Dennis breezed in, rubbing his hands at the thought of more food and commenting on how well he felt on such a pleasant morning. Arnie's hound-dog expression changed to one of distinct disapproval at this, and grew blacker when I asked Dennis if he had had a comfortable and restful night. I remember making a mental note to keep away from the water's edge during the day if Arnie was anywhere near.

The day produced some good fishing. We all caught fish — some very nice roach and bream — with the exception of Arnie who spent much of the day catching up on the sleep he had missed the previous night.

On our way home we called for the inevitable pint at a public house on the outskirts of Oakham. In conversation with the landlord, over a drink and some beautiful new crusty bread and stilton cheese for which the area is well known, he mentioned a reservoir close at hand which by reputation was good for fishing, although the implications of his remarks meant nothing to me until much later in my fishing career.

CHAPTER SIX

Some weeks later, while I was reading through the fishing catalogue acquired at Tom Watson's, I noticed that on the back page was a list of fishing clubs in the area, together with the names of the secretaries. One in particular caught my interest — the Derby Railway Institute — which offered waters for both coarse and trout fishing. I mentioned it to George and Arnie who were also excited by the idea and keen to pursue the possibilities of trout fishing. We called on Syd for advice, and he immediately informed us that he had been a member of the Derby Railway Club and that they had some very good trout water on the River Derwent in the north of Derbyshire. He went to great lengths to explain that fly fishing called for different rods, reels and lines from those required for coarse fishing and promised to give us a demonstration of his fly fishing tackle at Arnie's house one Sunday morning.

The rod he produced for our inaugural lesson was much shorter than ours and noticeably lighter. The line on his reel, which had a caged drum, was made of silk and very thick in comparison with our fine nylon. On the end of the thicker line coming from the reel he tied about eight feet of nylon of the type with which we were more familiar, passing this through the rod rings with the thicker line following. He then chose an imitation fly from the selection he had brought with him and attached it to the free end of the nylon. Once these preliminaries had been completed he began to demonstrate the technique of casting. He drew some line off the reel with one hand and then brought the rod to the vertical position with the other, which had the effect of sending the line out behind him in the air, level with the top of the rod. A deft movement forward with the forearm sent the line horizontally forward, again level with the top of the rod. As soon as the line was fully forward, up went the rod to its vertical position and back went the line, increasing in length as Syd released more line from the reel with his other hand. We were very impressed, standing there watching the line following its graceful air-borne path until there was some twenty feet of it extending from the tip of the rod, one second horizontally in front and the next horizontally behind. Syd's movements were quite unhurried as he stood there with his elbow close to his side, lifting the rod, which had become an extension of his forearm, to the vertical position. Without looking he knew exactly when the line was fully extended behind him and would send it forward with a minimal movement of arm and rod. Eventually he dropped his arm on the forward movement, allowing the fully extended line and fly to fall lightly on the grass of Arnie's lawn. He went on to tell us how essential it was to be able to cast a fly accurately at any distance. He showed us imitations of natural flies which hatch on our rivers and gave us information on some of the finer points of game fishing which made absorbing listening; although much of it was beyond our comprehension at the time, it really whetted our appetite for fishing the fly for trout.

After many anxious weeks of waiting, our application to join the Derby Railway Institute Fishing Club was eventually accepted. More frustrating delays followed, since the tickets ran from the sixteenth of June each year, which is the beginning of the coarse fishing season, and not the sixteenth of March which is the date for the beginning of the trout season. Consequently we had an agonising twelve weeks' wait until we could fish the waters on our new tickets.

During this time we carried on coarse fishing and, on reflection, it did give us time to gather some information on fly fishing from books and purchase some of the necessary equipment. Syd suggested that we should visit Foster's Tackle Shop in Ashbourne, which proved to be invaluable. Fly rods differ enormously, each one designed to carry a certain weight of line giving a perfect balance when the two are used together.

The advice given to us at Foster's left nothing to be desired, even though we eventually bought secondhand rods, reels and lines. They explained everything in detail and were painstaking in making sure we were well satisfied with our purchases. They told us that for the River Derwent a nine to ten foot rod would be suitable and showed us a fair selection. I finally chose one of nine foot six, made of fibreglass, and a compatible reel and line. Arnie's choice was very similar, although his rod was three inches shorter, while George deferred his selection of tackle until some time later. Walking out of the shop proudly and reverently clutching my prized yet comparatively modest purchases, I felt much as when I had acquired that first rod from Mr Hendy — excited almost to the point of being overcome with emotion.

We spent many hours on Arnie's lawn trying to master the art of casting so ably demonstrated by Syd. George eventually fixed himself up with a rod, line and reel and joined us for these practice sessions. It all looked so simple in the hands of an expert, but in the hands of novices proved very difficult. We found it hard to keep the line fluently airborne. If it was left too long in the air before changing direction it touched the ground either in front or at the back, or if it was reversed from one direction to another too quickly a sharp crack resulted, much the same as a coachman's whip, which had the effect of snapping the fly off the end of the nylon. It was during one of these sessions, when my line was cracking and snapping at nearly ever cast, that Arnie wryly suggested that one of my ancestors must have had stage coach experience. It did not help when people walking by stared in disbelief at the spectacle and made the obvious comment that we were never likely to catch anything there. After a few weeks we were able to keep the line in the air and extend the distance to some degree, with the cracks, tangles and removal of grass from the lawn becoming less frequent.

We discovered that the Derwent could be fished about three miles above Derby by obtaining a day ticket, and that there were trout as well as coarse fish in that particular stretch. But before we could try our new though still unperfected skills we needed other pieces of equipment. Information gleaned from books suggested that it was essential to wade into the river, so we would require thigh boots to replace the more familiar wellingtons and a landing net which could be carried on the person. Our nets were on long poles, enabling us to reach into the river from a sitting position or down to the water from some high bank — quite inappropriate for the more mobile game fisherman. We had to buy one or two flies which we finally selected on the basis of colour or the pleasant-sounding names mentioned by Syd, or from patterns listed in the books we had read, rather than from any first-hand knowledge or experience. We all bought a few leaders, the name given to the piece of nylon which extends from the thicker fly line to the fly.

Dennis, who had remained an observer of our latest venture, had produced — whence we did not ask — some thigh boots of the type worn by men who work in deep water cleaning out drains. These were not exactly fly fishing gear as seen in catalogues or on the best-dressed fly fishermen, but we were very grateful. I made some short aluminium handles to replace the long poles of our landing nets, and attached a piece of elastic to each of them by threading it through a hole I had drilled at the top. We could now sling these nets over our shoulders and adjust the length of the elastic so that they rested conveniently at our sides at waist height, not unlike a shoulder bag, at the same time

50

allowing them to stretch down to water level to land a fish if the need ever arose.

We went over the tackle repeatedly before setting off for the Derwent. Rods, reels, leaders, flies, thigh boots, landing nets were all checked, before we finally convinced ourselves that nothing had been overlooked.

When we arrived at the river we found that the nearest and most convenient place to park was under some trees by the roadside, just opposite the Bridge Inn at Duffield. The image we must have presented to anyone seeing us appear from behind the car as they passed by or sat taking refreshment in the Bridge Inn, makes me shudder when I think of it now. There we were, complete novices, dressed in old coats which hardly reached our new, shiny, black sewer boots, each with a landing net suspended from the shoulder with what could only be described as white knicker elastic, and trying to give the impression of game fishermen!

We hurried to the riverside as if we were expecting it to be suddenly spirited away, and quickly put the rods together, attached the reel, fastened the leader to the fly line and finally attached the fly. The sensation of wading stealthily into the river for the first time was unforgettable. It gave me a tremendous feeling of freedom, after so many hours of sitting by the water, to be actually walking about on the river bed feeling the movement and the pressure of water against my legs and the pebbles as they rolled away from underneath those large boots. The water was very clear, unlike the stretch we normally fished below Derby, which was discoloured by city and industrial waste. The bed of the river, with its pebbles and gravel, was in sharp contrast to the mud and silt only a few miles below.

After a few attempts at casting a fly I was suddenly conscious of George who was sitting on the bank watching.

'Why aren't you fishing?' I enquired.

'I've forgotten how to tie on a fly,' came the despondent and somewhat embarrassed reply.

The Bridge Inn at Duffield.

A few minutes later, after I had given him one or two instructions, he had once again mastered the half blood knot which is used to tie the fly to the leader, and began making his first attempts at casting from his position in the river.

It was difficult making the transition to casting in the open after the confines of a garden. We found that standing in the river made quite a difference. The depth of water elevated the point of contact of the fly and the surface was mobile compared with the stationary target of Arnie's lawn. As the fly alighted on the water it was instantly redirected towards us on the current at what seemed like an alarming rate of knots; loose line had to be retrieved in our free hands to keep in contact with the fly before casting again. But we persevered and learned much from our first experience of fly fishing. We did not see anything that vaguely resembled a trout 'rising to the surface leaving rings as it sipped a fly before returning to its original position', as described in the books we had read, and the landing nets were not required, but it did not seem to matter. We were actually out on a river which contained trout, in the peace and quiet of the Derwent, with the freedom to move easily and test our new techniques and equipment.

CHAPTER SEVEN

Our first sight of our fishing territory on the river above Matlock, determined by our tickets, left us feeling rather apprehensive. We had decided to reconnoitre the water before the sixteenth of June in order to familiarise ourselves with the area and the boundaries. We found one of the access points to be a track which led down to the river from the main Matlock-to-Bakewell road. It was awkward to negotiate with its bumps, ruts and overhanging foliage, and in many places only just wide enough for a car. I began to wonder whether we had found the correct track as the car lurched over the uneven ground and the grass clipped and scraped the undercarriage, but much to my relief it eventually opened out into a most picturesque car park on the river bank, shaded by the branches of a beautifully shaped tree. It was well worth the effort as we stood there in the valley, away from the road and civilisation, with only the Derwent and the Derbyshire hills for company. The river was crystal-clear as it meandered through the meadows, chattering as it swept over shallow gravel beds or very quiet when it passed through deeper pools where the weed wavered softly in the steady current. The air was noticeably fresh as we explored, tickets in hand, opened at the page which showed a map of the surroundings and the river clearly marked with the limits of how far we could fish and which also enclosed what in due course would be known affectionately as 'our' stretch of water. Each meadow was clearly marked, so it was not particularly difficult for us to find the boundaries up- or downstream from the car park, which was conveniently situated more or less in the centre of what must have been a two-mile stretch of river.

We walked the whole length, often pausing, and even with our limited experience pointed out what we assumed would be likely places to fish, or passively watched a mallard swim by followed by as many as ten young which resembled yellow and black balls of fluff, their legs working hard in a desperate attempt to keep in formation. Peace was shattered from time to time when a moorhen suddenly decided to break cover and hurry off upstream, half-flying, half-paddling, before splashing down at what it considered to be a safe distance.

There was so much to absorb on that first walk along the river that it did not occur to us until some time later, on our way back to the car, that amid all the activity we had not seen a single fish. We began to feel a little despondent as we travelled home, trying to find some constructive explanations. Did we know what a rising trout looked like? Surely we did. Even the small fish we had seen in ponds or canals left rings as they took some edible morsel from the surface of the water. Was it the right time of year? Could they still be feeding on the bottom as coarse fish do before the water

MALLARD

55

warms up? After all, it was not the height of summer and the water must still be relatively cold, coming as it did from the very north of Derbyshire. Was it that the river had very few fish or no fish at all? Whatever the reason, having bought tackle and tickets, we were not overjoyed at the prospect of fishing a fishless river, despite its beautiful and alluring setting. It is strange how on these occasions it is always the worst alternative which becomes uppermost in the mind. By the time we had reached home we were so dejected that we were considering selling the tackle and replacing it with tandems and taking up cycling as a hobby — until we saw the funny side.

During the week before the first Saturday of our permits, I decided to go straight from work to have another look at the Derwent. A complete transformation had taken place since our previous visit. I stood breathless and spellbound: for as far as I could see, the surface of the river was ringed with rising fish. Some were close to the bank, behind the roots growing from the trees at the water's edge; some were lying behind or at the side of the weed beds; while others were splashing in twos and threes in the more open water. The river was again alive — but this time with freely rising fish — as my eyes, which must have resembled the proverbial 'chapel hat pegs', darted from one place to another, attracted by the disturbances of movement and sound.

I made for the car at a run and drove back out of breath and with perspiration running down my face. It seemed vital to tell Arnie and George as quickly as possible about my discovery, and although I must certainly have exceeded the speed limit during that twenty miles, it seemed like an eternity before I was hammering on George's door. Arnie was summoned, and I vividly, and I hope without any exaggeration, related what I had seen.

It was early on Saturday morning when we loaded the boot, ready for the first of many journeys to the Derwent. Our excited conversation about the day's prospects helped the forty-minute journey to pass quickly. The possibility of not catching a fish was never mentioned at all, but speculations ran high as to how many we would catch, what size they would be and whether they would be trout or grayling. As we approached the river the car began to speed up, quite unconsciously on my part, as the thought of what lay ahead imparted extra pressure to the accelerator. We arrived at the gate to the track, and with much more confidence this time, followed it to the river where we were greeted with the sight of rising fish. It was an education for me to see the expressions on the faces of Arnie and George while they slowly digested what was happening, endorsing what I had described to them earlier in the week. For a long moment they watched mesmerised, almost in disbelief, before they broke into shouting and laughter as they pointed out various fish and their fascinating antics.

Suddenly it seemed essential to begin fishing immediately, and there was a disorganised and ungentlemanly attack on the contents of the car boot. We found ourselves bumping into each other, tripping over tussocks of grass and falling over the bags which had already been ejected from the car. At one point George and I were trying to remove the same wader which was see-sawing underneath one of the bags, with me pulling the boot end while he was pulling the top.

Arnie was between us, playing tug-of-war with a landing net which refused to move under the weight of other items.

'Just a minute,' ordered George in his more usual phlegmatic manner. 'Stand back, I'll see to it'.

A degree of calm and a sense of order was immediately restored to the proceedings. Even when all the contents had been placed on the grass and we began to change, Arnie found himself with two waders of different sizes, which was a good thing because George was having great difficulty trying to put his foot into one which was far too small. We could hear him muttering oaths under his breath and complaining that his socks were far too thick, before Arnie

The Car Park by the River Derwent.

suggested that he should try the one which was far too big for him. I, too, was experiencing wader trouble in my haste to change amid uncontrollable fits of laughter at George's expense, even though I had a left and a right and they were the correct size. Invariably my foot became stuck halfway down the boot while standing stork fashion on the other leg. Now, in my anxiety to force my foot down I pulled too hard, which had me hopping madly round the car park in an effort to keep upright, before I overbalanced and was left looking rather ungainly, with a boot half on while the other half lay on the ground at right angles to my now grounded foot. George had observed my circus act with some amusement and felt that honour had been restored when he nudged Arnie and pointed across to me, remarking on my peculiarly shaped extended leg.

At last we were changed, but we experienced further difficulties in setting up the rods through over-eagerness to be on the river and amongst the fish, which we could still see and hear from our vantage point in the car park. We were all fingers and thumbs, which did not help when trying to pass the fine, transparent nylon through the small rings on the rods before tying on the fly. In the end everything seemed ready, until Arnie realised that he had missed one of the rings, which meant removing the fly and rethreading his line. Why, when hours of fishing lay ahead, everything had to be done so quickly and urgently, I could not understand, unless we imagined that the fish would suddenly move into another territory or that the whole river would be unexpectedly taken over by other fishermen.

George went up the river from the car and disappeared into the distance at great speed. Arnie decided to stay near the car and have a pipe of tobacco to observe what was happening and, presumably, to calm his nerves. I selected an area some fifty or so yards above the car, where I had seen many fish rising during my previous visit. After carefully taking up my position in the river there must have been

59

twenty or so fish rising in front of me. I made desperate efforts to land my fly lightly on the water in the hope that one of them would mistake my artificial offering for the real thing. The more I fished the more absorbing and frustrating it became; either through my over-eagerness or through annoying gusts of wind, which always seemed to blow at the most inconvenient time, the fly persistently chose its own course and place to land, sometimes several feet away from the spot I had intended in order that it might float down towards and over a rising fish. Sometimes, through bad manipulation of the rod, the line would land on the water in a heap and with a horrible splash, which stopped many fish rising for a time. Now and again the fly would land in what I considered the perfect place, only to be dragged away from its proper course by the line when it caught the current on its way back to me. Even if by chance the fly floated over one of those numerous fish, they showed no interest whatsoever in my offering.

George suddenly appeared from somewhere upstream and watched my efforts for a while before informing me that it was time for lunch: we had arranged to meet at the car at one o'clock. I looked in disbelief at my watch, which read one-fifteen. I had spent just over three hours riveted to that one place, so enthralled that the minutes had evaporated and the passage of time had become quite irrelevant. As we recalled the events of the morning over tomatoes and pieces of pork pie, it emerged that Arnie, too, had stayed more or less in one spot, as had George, which meant that although we had two miles of river, we had fished only three small areas.

Our desire to return to the battle destroyed our normal appetite, and it was not long before George and I were heading off upstream to our respective areas of river, again leaving Arnie to renew his attempts at the fish close to the car. I asked George if he would like to try his luck in the stretch of the river where I had spent so much time during the morning. 'No, thanks, see you later,' he said rather abruptly as he marched off with a determined and measured tread, obviously intent on resuming his acquaintance with the fish that he had spent so much time wooing during the morning. The afternoon proved to be more or less a repeat of the morning — plenty of fish rising but proving impossible to catch due to their lack of interest in the several fly patterns I offered; or due to my combined lack of knowledge, experience and skill. The latter, as I realise now, was closer to the truth.

During this session I found my concentration becoming increasingly divided between fishing and an awareness of my surroundings. The comical antics of the water voles particularly caught my eye. They would suddenly appear from underwater, carrying weed in large quantities across to one side of the river or the other, which was usually a prelude to a wrestling match when they tried to persuade the weed to enter one of their many holes in the bank. Emerging victorious, they would sit on their hind legs preening and sunning themselves and, after what looked like a brief period of self-congratulation, would set off for more weed and a

WATER VOLE

further struggle. The moorhens and mallards had a graceful charm of their own, providing they were not disturbed by humans or engaged in defending their territory against other aquatic intruders. At times it was pleasant just to stand or sit breathing the fresh, clean air, watching the clouds painting patterns on the hillsides as they temporarily obscured the sun, and thinking how grateful and privileged I was to be part of such an environment.

During a break for further refreshment later in the afternoon, three more fishermen came into view, working their way slowly and methodically upstream towards us. One would cast a fly over a fish leaving the other two to move further forward. This progression was repeated several times until they came up level with us. The way they manipulated the rod, line and fly was a pleasure to watch. Up went the rod, back went the line, and a quick flick of the arm propelled the line across the whole width of the river, letting the fly land lightly no more than a foot in front of a rising trout. If the trout did not respond the line was lifted off the water and effortlessly returned to within an inch or so of the first cast, with little fuss, no splash but great accuracy. This they repeated several times before moving to the next fish. It was an experience and a joy for us to witness such a display of grace, precision and totally co-ordinated movement, and although it left me feeling rather inadequate by comparison, it made me more determined than ever to perfect my technique and gain the necessary knowledge so that one day I could emulate their expertise. It was obvious that George and Arnie were impressed as they made comments like, 'Bloody hell, did you see that?' or, 'Just look at that!' as though my back had been turned or my interest distracted by something else at the time. 'I'll never be able to cast like that,' George informed us. I will, I thought, walking back to what was now called 'my spot' on the river. It did occur to me, as I made more efforts to persuade the line and fly to follow my mechanical instructions, that it might take some time.

The fishing inevitably dominated our conversation during the journey back and over a pint at the Chequers, which was gradually becoming a Fishing as well as a Cricket Clubhouse. As the evening drew to a close, the talk about our first day on the Derwent became increasingly punctuated with yawns as the fresh air and the exertions of the day began to take their toll.

CHAPTER EIGHT

The more we visited the Derwent, which was every Saturday, the more enjoyable it became, as our casting improved and we began to feel more at home on the river, although we did not see very much of it. We were still obsessed by the areas of river we had first selected, as though they were the only three worthwhile places to be, and headed for them as soon as possible after our arrival. It was a major catastrophe if another fisherman looked to be heading that way and we would wait with bated breath until he either stopped short or by-passed what we considered to be 'ours'.

My initial awkward casting movements, which often resulted in an aching wrist and arm, were becoming far less of a strain on limbs and patience as my technique gradually improved. I felt more relaxed, self-assured and confident. It began to *feel* right and I would increasingly sense when the fly would be presented properly. I watched Arnie from time to time and noticed that his efforts, too, were becoming less laboured, with a resulting marked increase in both distance and accuracy. George could seldom be found, so we could only rely on his say-so to assess his progress, but he seemed to be happy.

The three we had watched so intently and enviously on our first visit appeared every Saturday at some time or another. The first week or so produced the usual exchange of courtesies, but as the weeks went by these were followed by longer conversations about the state of the river, the fly hatch and how many fish had been caught. We soon learned that Jack and Cyril always travelled together from Derby while Fred came from Nottingham, mostly on his own unless his brother, who did not fish, decided to join him for a walk down the river.

Gradually, as we became more accepted, they began to offer us advice on where to fish and give us information on what particular fly patterns to use according to the time of day and the season of the year. Names like March Brown, Blue Dun, Steel Blue, Greenwell's Glory and Ginger Quill spring quickly to mind. They also impressed on us that what they told us would not guarantee results, although it might help. This was very welcome because although we now felt competent to cast a fly adequately and more often than not with a reasonable degree of accuracy, our fly patterns did not hold any fascination for the trout. We had seen Jack, Cyril and Fred catch one or two fish or at least have fish rising to their fly on occasions, so once we had purchased some of their recommended patterns we would feel much more confident.

The more authoritative our talk about fishing sounded, the more interested and involved Syd became, until at last he suggested a few days' fishing on the River Ure at Borough-bridge in Yorkshire. He knew the area well from his wanderings throughout the country and described in great detail the delights of fishing from a particular weir on the river, which produced exceptionally large barbel; it was, he said, a delightful spot, set in the grounds of a large estate. It also contained trout, giving us a choice of either coarse or game fishing, which was ideal in our transition stage and would also make it possible for Dennis, who was keen to go, to do some fishing despite his lack of game fishing gear. I was pleased to learn from Syd that maggots could be obtained from a tackle shop in Boroughbridge, which would eliminate any risk of a repeat of our boot-clearing episode while we were fishing on the Ouse.

It was about seven o'clock when I arrived at George's on the morning of departure. Arnie was already there, sitting next to George on the wall outside the house, surrounded and half-hidden by an enormous array of tackle. There were rods, fishing baskets, boxes, flasks, waders, trout bags, landing nets and cases; it all looked far too much for the boot, which was already carrying my gear. George, however, was methodical and meticulous in the way he packed and made things disappear into the boot; he had a knack of fitting articles into holes left by cases and bags of unequal size — a coat here, a flask there, followed by an odd pair of socks — which not only stowed all the gear, but by the time he had finished everything was packed and secured to prevent noise or damage from untoward movement.

Syd arrived with Dennis and after a minimal exchange of pleasantries we set off for Yorkshire. We travelled up the M1, branching off for the M18 and then on to the Doncaster by-pass, before we turned off for Boroughbridge, roughly a hundred miles away — approximately an hour and a half's drive. The monotony of the journey was relieved by our excited chatter which, if it had been recorded, would have sounded more appropriate to a bunch of overgrown school-boys discussing their first encounter with the opposite sex, than to a group of what could only be described as older men. I must confess that there is very little difference now, some twenty years later, when I am preparing and setting off for a few days' fishing to places old or new, and I hope there never will be, otherwise a love affair with fishing and all its peripheral rewards will be over.

We quickly checked into the hotel where we had booked all single rooms this time — at Arnie's insistence — before following Syd to the tackle shop for the rod licences, because as well as requiring them for the area, we thought we would show Dennis what they looked like for future reference. We also purchased some maggots, although in much more conservative quantities than on our last trip, even taking Dennis's extravagance into account!

From there we went to the Estate Office for the permits

before heading for the river on roads which left the town three or four miles behind and became more and more rural. Syd turned off and drove through some large, very ornate wrought iron gates and into parkland of the type one sees in the grounds of stately homes. I became distinctly uneasy when I noticed pheasants strutting about looking quite unperturbed and very tolerant of our presence, which suggested to me unaccustomed intrusion. Judging by their lack of conversation and furtive glances, George and Arnie must have been having similar thoughts, as if they were expecting to be apprehended and accused of trespass. We were very relieved when Syd left the main drive, which by then was heading for a large stone mansion with manicured gardens and lawns, and followed a secondary drive which eventually led us to the edge of a wood. He jumped out of his car happily chattering and obviously quite at home, which allayed our fears to some extent.

'This is the closest we can take the cars,' he informed us as he began unloading his boot, whistling merrily, only stopping to add that the river was a short walk through the woods; he was apparently completely unaware of our earlier apprehension.

George continued in his role of 'baggage master' as he emptied my boot and divided the contents into three neat piles. We must have looked like a line of loaded pack-horses as we trooped through the woods, having negotiated one of those infuriating iron gates that swing in a quadrant. This fiendish type of barrier will let you in willingly, but seems very reluctant to release you, particularly when a hand is not available to manipulate the swinging part. This usually leaves the irate negotiator wedged in the middle by the stomach and backside, which becomes the only part available to push the thing to its original position. To make matters worse, this usually has to be done on tip-toe, since the items being carried have to be manoeuvred over the top. I often wonder if the person who designed or installed such a system had a hide close by where he could observe the discomfort, frustration and anger, or listen to the language it provoked, in order to satisfy an unusual if not warped sense of humour.

During the walk through the wood I noticed rustic archways from time to time, and for much of the way there was ageing trellis-work attempting to hold back several varieties of overgrown shrubs and unruly bushes. Much of it was in a state of disrepair and looked resigned, after many long and faithful years, to losing its battle with the advancing foliage. I assumed that the wood must have been landscaped with the rest of the grounds and tried to imagine how it had looked in its prime, with the Lord and Lady or their guests taking an early morning or late evening stroll. I began to wonder who had graced this path and how many had been favoured by the setting it provided.

I was abruptly awakened from my reverie by the sight of the river which suddenly appeared, forming a neat, meandering boundary to the woods. It was fairly wide, with a weir stretching out immediately in front of us. The water dropped some fifteen feet to our left, at an angle of about forty-five degrees, then flowed over a level area of concrete and dropped a further twelve vertical inches into a pool before resuming its more natural journey to the sea. The water behind the weir appeared to be deep and quiet but the speed as it cascaded down the man-made obstacle was quite an alarming sight, despite its lack of depth. Syd waded into the water and began to walk across the top of the weir.

'Where the hell is he going now?' asked Arnie with more than a hint of alarm in his voice.

Before we could answer, Syd beckoned from the middle of the river, looking quite surprised at our reluctance to follow. I do not know whether it was bravado, complete confidence in Syd, an urgency to begin fishing or sheer lunacy which prompted George to set off on what seemed a foolhardy walk across the river. Normally George had a measured and purposeful tread, but on this occasion he progressed rather slowly and in a manner which I can only describe as a furtive shuffle. If George can do it so can I, I thought to myself, and after taking a deep breath I dropped onto the weir from the bank and began a slow, nervous progress. Arnie immediately followed, keeping very close to me and no doubt working on the theory of safety in numbers. The crossing looked worse than it was, with the water no more than a few inches deep for the entire length, but standing in the middle at the point of no return, looking down with trepidation towards the base of the weir, we realised that our fear was magnified by the speed of the water.

By the time Dennis had joined us Syd had pretty well tackled up. The strange thing was that he had accomplished this sitting in a tubular-framed chair of brightly coloured canvas, of the type normally associated with sunbathing on the lawn or on a beach. Our own aids to comfort were the usual fishing baskets which held much of our incidental tackle and acted as a seat when most of the contents had been removed. It was only when Syd began fishing that the advantages of his seating arrangements became evident. He told us the best place to fish was from the concrete platform at the bottom of the weir, where the speed of water, particularly in flood conditions, had gouged a deep hole beyond the weir and where many fish congregated in well-oxygenated water.

With chair in one hand and rod in the other, he made his way down to the base of the weir and was soon sitting in armchair comfort in the middle of the concrete platform, casting into the pool. We began to realise that on this occasion our fishing baskets would be quite inadequate, as the water, although only an inch or so deep, would flow through the holes in the wicker-work. Syd's answer to standing, in the form of a sunchair allowing the water to flow over the metal frame and well below the seat, was very effective.

It was not long before we were all spaced out at regular intervals along the weir, keenly watching our respective floats as they bobbed and turned in the current and turbulence of the water beyond. I was fascinated as I watched the way the agitation of the river controlled these movements. One minute the float would be stationary close by, the next it would be following a circular path or dancing off downstream as the eddies and boils determined its course.

The woods we had walked through were now high on our left, providing a beautiful leafy backdrop to the river. The bank on our right was more open but quite high, which made the whole area a perfect suntrap. We were soon in shirt-sleeves enjoying the sun and very grateful to have the cooling effect of the water passing over our waders.

While I was still lost in admiration of the scenery, my float suddenly disappeared. The next moment I was having a tremendous battle with a fish in the depths of the pool, of a weight and power which I had never encountered before. I remember feeling somewhat apprehensive and at the same time excited at what was underneath the surface, as the fish fought for its freedom, using the currents and eddies to supplement its own powerful movements. Syd's voice seemed very distant when he told me that it might well be one of the large barbel associated with the area. Time becomes totally meaningless on these occasions and the presence of other people fades into obscurity as the fight continues.

Eventually the fish began to tire, which enabled me to bring it closer to the surface and get a glimpse of it as it looped, dived and swirled, causing the rod to jerk, bend, straighten and bend again in response, echoing the erratic, explosive actions of the fish. Only when its frantic efforts to escape had subsided did I become aware of George standing close by with his net poised, ready to land the fish, which we accomplished after it had made one final effort to release itself from the hook with a powerful shake of its head. Sure enough, it was a barbel weighing some three and a half pounds, which the others admired almost to the point of reverence. The size was mentioned several times as were the condition and the colour, in tones of wondering delight. Naturally I was overjoyed at catching the largest fish of my career so far, but once it had been landed it was something of an anticlimax compared with the fight it had given me.

During the rest of the morning we caught several more fish. Arnie was very fearful of a large perch he landed, which repeatedly raised its poisonous dorsal fin, making handling difficult. Much advice was proffered but I noticed that no one was prepared to give any practical help. George and Dennis caught some roach, all larger than average, and I managed two more barbel; it was an enthralling morning's fishing.

We had decided to return to Boroughbridge for lunch, which meant another shuffle across the top of the weir. We accomplished this with a little more confidence than the first time and not quite so slowly, but it struck me that the noisy chatter ceased until we had reached the safety of the opposite bank. We retraced our steps through the woods, which provided temporary shade from the burning sun. Once at the cars, Syd and Dennis led the way back to the town. We three were following quite happily, when Syd's car suddenly veered off to the right and onto the opposite grass verge, braking quickly in a cloud of dust. When we drew level with them they smiled and gesticulated that all was well, so we carried on until we found ourselves on a large roundabout on the outskirts of town.

'Which way?' I asked.

'Don't know,' came the reply from the back, in a manner which lacked any concern for my predicament.

'Thanks,' I said, before realising that there was little I could do but stay on the roundabout and try to pick up the Boroughbridge sign. Just as I was approaching one road rather slowly, looking for the sign and receiving little help from my tired and hungry friends, I recognised the car coming onto the roundabout in front of me as Syd's. As soon as he saw me he realised, judging by the laughter, that

I was about to begin a second circuit. As we followed once again I could see him shaking with laughter in his customary demonstrative manner, with Dennis turning round making circular movements with his hands, as if to suggest that another circuit might be in order. It took many years for me to live down the saga of the Boroughbridge roundabout.

When we arrived at the restaurant car park Syd almost fell out of the car with tears streaming down his face and his hands clutching his ribs.

'Just a minute!' I retaliated. 'What was the idea of driving across the road?' He calmed down enough to explain, with the aid of Dennis, that a wasp had entered the car and it was that which had caused the temporary diversion.

After lunch and an uneventful return to the river (with a noticeably quicker, almost contemptuous walk across the weir), we began another session fishing the pool. The heat by this time was almost unbearable. The water sparkled as the irregularities in its surface reflected the sun, and the silk weed shone like an emerald carpet on the declivity of the weir. After a time Syd decided to take an afternoon siesta, while Arnie set up a fly rod and went for a walk down river at a very leisurely, almost lethargic pace. George, Dennis and I were quite content to stay by the weir fishing, chatting or just sitting absorbing the peace and serenity of the place. It never ceases to amaze me how the slightest movements become exaggerated in these languorous conditions. A bird hopping from one branch to another, a water vole sitting upright or a mallard beginning to preen, suddenly becomes the focus of attention amongst the panorama of inactivity.

As the sun began to descend towards the horizon, casting longer shadows and a softer light, we returned to the weir and more serious fishing resumed. Syd arose from his slumbers and Arnie appeared from his sojourn down the river and immediately hooked and landed a very nice grayling. The river provided more sport until it was time to return to the hotel for the evening meal. This was of course preceded by cryptic references to the number of circuits of the round-about I would need and whether Syd would make another attempt to find a short cut across the fields.

Five very bronzed, contented but hungry fishermen sat down to the evening meal before retiring to the bar to complete a memorable day. Our conversation during the evening naturally enough reflected the events of the day and was quite rational until tiredness and the number of pints consumed gradually began to take their toll. I think the conversation really began to deteriorate when Arnie tried to convince everyone, including the locals who seemed to be enjoying our company, that the monstrous perch he had caught actually attacked him with those poisonous spikes on the tips of its dorsal fin. Syd's eyes again began to water and his whole body shook like an unrestrained pneumatic drill as he tried to describe how he felt when he saw my car on its second circuit of the roundabout, although I did subdue him temporarily when I made the observation, somewhat noisily I suspect, that our venerable guide was the only one of the party who had not caught a fish and that even Dennis, a relative novice, had managed several good fish, which was much to his credit. This immediately prompted Dennis to buy another round.

It was midnight before George suggested that unless we had some sleep we would be in poor condition to fish in the morning. After several 'Goodnights' to the landlord, who I am sure would have kept the bar open all night if required, we staggered off to our respective rooms.

The following morning I woke up feeling dreadful, with an awful headache and a horrible taste in my mouth. It was an effort to rise, even for the early morning tea which had arrived. I had better not let the others know how I feel, I thought, as I made intermittent attempts to get dressed after a relatively sobering wash in cold water. I had to keep sitting down on the bed, leaning forwards in the numb recovery position of head in hands, vowing never to touch another

73

drop, in between putting clothes onto parts of my body which did not seem to belong entirely to me. A walk in the fresh air would be the best thing, I thought, although the effort even that required made the prospect seem somewhat forbidding. Conquering the inclination to creep back into bed, I made my way downstairs, hoping to avoid the others. The last thing I needed was a hale and hearty 'Good morning' and a reminder of what a splendid night it had been.

I decided to walk to the road-bridge which crossed the river. The fresh air had the desired effect, and I began to feel much better until I reached the bridge and looked down into the water. Watching the river rushing beneath at great speed brought on further bouts of dizziness; the whole bridge felt as if it were moving upstream propelled by some impalpable force which had me holding on to the parapet for dear life. I felt as though the water was drawing me towards it, so I quickly if somewhat shakily retreated from the bridge and returned to face breakfast back at the hotel. How I was going to tackle a fried breakfast without letting on how I felt was going to be difficult. Even the thought of a greasy egg evoked a feeling of nausea.

Syd was sitting in the lounge behind a newspaper when I walked in.

'Morning, how are you?' I enquired as heartily as possible.

'Fine, thanks, lovely morning,' came the reply.

I almost believed him, until I noticed that the large headlines on the paper were upside down.

George appeared next, looking as if a trip to the opticians would not do him any harm, followed by Arnie who grunted what we assumed to be 'Good morning'. Dennis breezed in just as he had done at Ely, commenting on the pleasant morning and saying that he was ready for a good breakfast. I find this breed of person, who always appears looking bright and cheerful early in the morning, apparently immune to the effects of the revelries of the night before, quite infuriating, although I am sure it is pure envy on my part.

Breakfast was a quiet affair compared with the meal of the previous evening. I knew how I felt and what the cause was, and although I had a shrewd idea of how everyone else, with the exception of Dennis, might be feeling, pride prevented me from admitting to such weakness before close friends and self-confessed connoisseurs of a good pint. Dennis ordered a full house after the usual cereal or fruit juice, and we all followed his lead. The thought of egg, bacon, sausage and tomato left me in some doubt about the wisdom of putting on such a brave face, but the more I managed to eat the better I began to feel, and by the end of the meal I felt quite human again.

Every time the waitress arrived Arnie's face took on a distinctly sheepish look which George responded to very quickly. 'What's the matter?' he asked. Arnie became very embarrassed, and went on to tell us that because the night was so warm and humid he had been sleeping on top of the bed completely naked and was still in that position when he heard a knock on the door. Assuming it to be one of us he did not bother retreating under the covers. By the time he drowsily realised it was the lady with the early morning tea, who was now serving our breakfast, there was very little he could do to regain his dignity. His embarrassment was complete when our waitress pointedly waited to serve him last and, with a slight blush and an impish grin, bowed politely before presenting Arnie with his plate, which held an extra sausage!

* * *

Another day's fishing meant another visit to the estate office for the permits, which we left to Syd since he knew the routine well from previous visits. In our anxiety to be down on the river this exercise always seemed to take an agonisingly long time, but on this occasion Syd was out of the office within seconds. We bombarded him with questions.

'I can't stay in there,' he gasped. 'One of you will have to go, the room's spinning and the ceiling's coming down.' When George described the office with its low-beamed ceiling we realised that the previous night had affected Syd more than he was prepared to say.

We were soon down by the river, setting up the tackle for another session on the weir. Syd was a long way behind the rest of us and obviously in difficulty. I left my position and went to see what sort of trouble he was in. Everything seemed to be in order until I saw him making valiant attempts to attach a hook to the end of the nylon. He knew what to do but his trembling hands made the task impossible. I thought it gentlemanly not to mention the previous evening or the upside-down paper or the episode in the estate office, as I tied on the hook for him. He made his way deliberately down to the weir; no sooner had he cast into the pool than his rod bent under a terrific strain, much to the disgust of Arnie, George and Dennis, who by now had been fishing for some time. The parabolic arc of the rod remained unmoving and their disgust soon changed to amusement when they realised that poor Syd, after all the trials and tribulations of the morning, had snagged the bottom. Eventually the line snapped and I found myself tying a second hook in place.

About ten minutes elapsed before Syd was once again leaving his position on the river, this time in rather a hurry.

'What's the matter now?' asked Dennis.

Without answering Syd dropped his rod on the bank and made his way hastily across the top of the weir, disappearing quickly into the woods. It was a relieved-looking Syd who reappeared shortly afterwards, and when we questioned him about his sudden disappearance he would only say that he felt much better, although rather concerned for the welfare of the pheasants should they ever go scratching about in that part of the wood.

When all the extraneous activity had subsided we began to

catch one or two fish. George and Arnie both caught fair-sized barbel as well as the more familiar roach and perch, but it was Dennis who really enjoyed himself, not only catching more fish but politely offering his spot to Syd who was still trying desperately to catch a fish of any description — although I suspect Dennis made this gracious gesture with tongue in cheek, judging by the roguish look on his face.

The day followed much the same pattern as the previous one, with all the fish being caught before the sun was at its height. After lunch we again relaxed, enjoying a doze or a chat or simply sitting gratefully contemplating the undisturbed beauty of natural things. I gazed at a branch that had been torn off by one of winter's gale-force winds, and now formed an obstruction in the water, creating irregular, poetic movement. How long had it been there? I wondered. Would it still be there if I ever visited the river again? Or would it have been washed away in a flood, only to come to rest further down river as the water subsided?

Our evening meal was fish and chips which we smuggled into the hotel and up to Arnie's room, he being the one who had drawn the short straw. Afterwards we left him wondering how he was going to destroy the evidence as we made our way down to the bar. Our intake of the local brew was very modest, nobody being willing to set the hectic pace of twenty-four hours earlier, although it was again gone midnight before we had finished reminiscing about our experiences of the last two days.

The following morning I decided to walk in on Arnie, aided and abetted by the others. I entered his room with a flourish, after a quick knock on the door, but he had learnt his lesson and I found him covered from chin to toe, and with a smile on his face which suggested that he was expecting just such an entrance.

Syd was not in a particularly good mood when he joined us for breakfast, which was quite out of character for him.

We had been placed at a table which he considered far too small for the comfort of five men. He summoned the head waiter who listened sympathetically to his grievances and promptly moved us to a larger table. We supported his actions to some extent, although we could not help feeling that his displeasure had something to do with the fact that he was obliged to leave us early that morning to visit some factory in the area on business, while we could still look forward to at least a morning's fishing before returning south. We asked for the bill to avoid a further visit to the hotel later in the day, which would enable us to begin our journey home straight from the river. Syd insisted that he would pay his part of the bill separately. We could not understand this at the time, because we had all had similar rooms and the same meals; it seemed logical to have one bill, to save the receptionist's time, with one person paying the whole amount, leaving us to sort out our finances at our own convenience.

We packed our cases and loaded them in the car. Syd appeared looking immaculate in a suit, ready for the business of the day, in sharp contrast to his more casual leisure attire. His lively chatter and jovial approach to life had been suddenly transformed into a rather subdued, businesslike manner as he checked the samples he needed for demonstration. To the accompaniment of our commiserations and farewells he drove reluctantly out of the car park.

While we were fishing during the morning Dennis suddenly exclaimed, 'The crafty beggar, I know why he wanted to pay his bill separately from ours. He's had a couple of days' fishing in the firm's time and they will be paying the bill.' We all wondered how many times this had happened on his travels around the country while presumably on business, and we were still speculating about it as we drove back to the Midlands after we had enjoyed the best of the morning's fishing.

CHAPTER NINE

We always looked forward eagerly to our Saturday fishing outings on the Derwent, and on Friday nights in the Chequers, amid the rattle of the dominoes, there would invariably be a discussion about the prospects for the following day. We would try to estimate the river level if rain had fallen during the week, and the possible strength of the wind, the one thing above all else that made fly fishing uncomfortable, dangerous or sometimes completely impossible.

One morning we decided to take the country route, where the road winds and twists through a patchwork of fields, their boundaries determined by the miles and miles of hand-built Derbyshire stone walls. We passed through the sleepy villages of Middleton-by-Wirksworth and Winster, avoiding the main road to Matlock Bath and Matlock, which was usually busy and slow-moving, with cars full of people descending on those central beauty spots of Derbyshire. As we were driving over the hills, the windscreen of the car became covered with flies — hundreds of black, white and red spots, as if we were suddenly moving through a shower of coloured rain. The windscreen washers provided only temporary relief, more bodies landing to impair our vision as fast as they were removed by the wiper blades and copious amounts of water.

Even though we had travelled what we now called the 'back way' to the river, it still meant a brief encounter with the busy road above Matlock. It was very gratifying to turn off and confidently follow our now familiar track, with each rut, dip and bump subconsciously noted as it led us to the river, and a quiet, noticeably different world. It had become a ritual to pause before we set up the rods to survey the river for tell-tale signs of its height, indicated by well-known boulders, and for the clarity which was determined by how much of the weed or pebbles we could see on the bottom. Many times we stood there, dismayed and despondent, looking out onto a high, chocolate-coloured river boiling and heaving with excess water, its surface carrying debris lifted from the margins as it rose, swollen by streams, dykes and land drains high up in the hills.

Very little rain had fallen during the previous week, so our initial surveillance confirmed the water to be in good condition, with many fish already rising quite freely; George lost no time in unpacking the fishing tackle from the boot. While I was setting up my rod and threading the line through the rings, the vision of all those flies on the windscreen kept returning and in particular the tiny red spots. This prompted me to select from the flies I had bought, on the advice of Jack and Cyril, a pattern called the 'Iron Blue'. As its name suggests, this is a fly tied with a grey-blue hackle to represent the wings, and mole fur to represent the body which is also a slate grey-blue in colour. The interesting thing to me was

HACKLE: BLUE DUN

BODY: MOLE FUR WITH RED TAG

TAIL: BLUE DUN FIBRES

IRON BLUE DUN

that at the back of the body of this particular fly pattern was a bright red tag which suggested the spots on the windscreen. My selection of fly, therefore, was determined by what had happened in the hills during our drive to the river rather than by any scientific study or observation of the river as the books advise. I did not look to see what type of flies were floating on the water, agitating and drying their wings before taking off and flying into the trees to mate; later in the evening the females would return to the river to lay their eggs, so ensuring the future of the species, before they died and floated off into oblivion.

It always strikes me as a little sad to think that the eggs will only live on the river bed for about a year, changing to nymphs before rising to the surface, where they emerge into adult flies. After a brief aerial honeymoon, the males die and the females return to the water within a day, to lay the eggs for another year, before dying in their turn. Many do not even complete this short and seemingly unfair cycle, being eaten by trout either on their way to the surface or on the surface itself as they dry their wings; or being eagerly snapped up as soon as they are airborne by the bullfinch, chaffinch, wagtail and swallow who instinctively know when a good fly hatch is imminent. The appearance of swallows from apparently nowhere, diving, wheeling, chattering and skimming the water at breath-taking speed, providing an absorbing display of aerobatics, is always a good indication of the intensity of a fly hatch on a river.

Armed with my 'Iron Blue', I made for my usual place on the river accompanied by George, leaving Arnie by the car. After a while I paused to watch several fish rising along the side of a weed bed, the tips of which were rhythmically swaying on the surface and gently disturbing the otherwise calm, flat area of water. The river was much deeper here and consequently moved much more slowly than in my usual spot. The fish rose leisurely and sedately, the river giving them more time to select their diet than those which were

Swallow skimming the water.

having to rise quickly and energetically in streamy water which accelerated as it cascaded through pebble banks and between boulders.

'I'm going to stay here for a while,' I said to George.

'Fine,' he replied. He then courteously asked if it was all right to fish what had come to be regarded as my spot round the corner.

'Sure,' I said.

He must be gaining in confidence, I thought, to be fishing in a place where he could be easily observed. He usually disappeared to some obscure part of the river, not to be seen again until our prearranged time for refreshment.

Intently I watched the fish rising persistently by the weeds and considered how best to gain access to the river and reach a position where it would be possible to cast a fly over them. The water was almost to the top of my waders as I slowly edged my way across, through a gully which had been formed by constant erosion over many years. Progress was not made any easier by having to walk on tip-toe through the deepest part, to avoid the water spilling over my fully extended waders, and I felt very insecure when the water pressure began to dislodge pebbles from underneath my feet which were already lacking maximum grip. After a few more nervous seconds the worst was over: I was in the middle of the river in much shallower water and feeling considerably more comfortable as I inched towards the weeds, trying not to create too much wave.

It was some time before I was casting in the general direction of the fish, increasing the length of line before dropping the fly onto the surface, where it rested temporarily until it started floating down on the current and over the approximate area of the fish. It was much easier to retrieve line and actually observe the fly in the slower water than in the faster shallows. Ah, that's about right, I thought after a few more attempts, when the fly landed very close to the weeds before sailing down the river like some miniaturised boat. A sudden swirl made my pulse race as a fish rose underneath my fly. I did not make contact but it was the first time a fish had shown any interest in what I had presented. My hands began to tremble and my heart was pounding with excitement, which made it difficult to regain any sort of co-ordination for a while. This, together with my extreme anxiety to place a fly in exactly the same position, made me revert to the hurried movements of my first efforts at casting, losing distance, accuracy and the ability to land a fly lightly and delicately onto the water. The fly landed clumsily and with a splash, but fortunately it was not close enough to frighten the fish away from its feeding place to the safety of the weeds, or to the bottom of the river out of harm's way.

When my composure had been somewhat restored, casting a fly into the right place once more became easier. There it was again. I saw the fly land lightly on the surface of the river above the fish. I watched it float slowly down towards the weeds. I was totally engrossed, hardly daring to breathe. 'Take it, take it,' I whispered as it passed over the rising trout. Sure enough, much to my delight it disappeared in a sudden, dramatic swirl. I quickly lifted the rod and felt the line tighten as the hook made contact with the fish with a heart-stopping thump.

The speed at which the fish cavorted about the river as it made furious attempts to shed the fly was quite alarming. It went to the left and then to the right before boring down towards the bed of the river, taking line so quickly that it made the reel scream. Then it rose to the top, breaking the surface with an almighty leap before splashing down to cut more erratic zig-zag paths across the river. It seemed an eternity before it began to tire and I could start to retrieve some of the line, gradually bringing the fish towards me. The efforts he was making were less powerful now and the looping runs and dives were becoming less frequent, which gave me the opportunity to unclip my landing net and lower it into the water. He came closer and closer before making one last desperate run when he saw the waiting net. I eased him slowly back until I could see his shadowy shape lying directly over the net. I can't lose him now, I thought, as I quickly lifted the net clear of the water, and felt very relieved to see that it contained a thrashing trout. I felt quite numb for a while until the reality of what I had just achieved slowly began to dawn. I found myself repeatedly looking at the fish in an attempt to reassure myself that I had indeed recorded my first trout and that it had not after all been just a dream. Of course it was real. I could feel the water pressing against my waders. I could feel the weight of the fish in the net, and I could measure the effects of anxiety, tension and concentration by the perspiration on my forehead, the rapid rate of my breathing and the weakness in my knees.

I was abruptly woken from my thoughts by the realisation that I needed to remove the fly from the fish and return him to the water after showing him to George, who was just round the corner. I could not accomplish this while standing in the river holding both rod and net, which meant that I had to return to the bank through the deep gully. Unfortunately I could not see the precise point at which I had entered the water because the bank appeared so very different when I looked at it from my position in the river. I tried in several places to get through, but each time the water was far too deep and it was even more difficult with my rod in one hand and the net and the fish in the other. There was only one thing to do: I made a desperate attempt to stride quickly over the gully and step onto the shallow side near the bank — with disastrous consequences. Down I went into the gully. At first the water did not seem to be entering my waders, but they were half-full before I managed to climb out and reach the safety of the bank.

Quickly I unhooked the fish and squelched round the corner to show George my first 'brownie'. It was a beautiful fish, as most brown trout are, with a white underside shading to olive green, turning to a golden brown on its back, with orange spots arranged in neat patterns along its sides. George was delighted. We stood there for some time admiring the sleek, shiny form glistening and glinting in the sun, before I walked down the bank and, with one last, lingering look, returned him carefully and ceremoniously to the water.

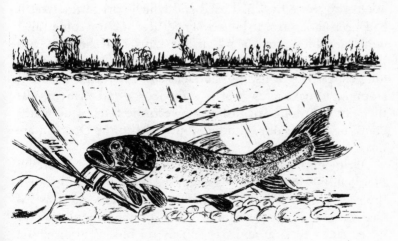

BROWN TROUT

85

The fact that I had caught a fish gave George fresh heart. He wanted to know what fly I had used and immediately changed to the pattern I eagerly described. While he was changing his fly, I explained that although the fish was only a modest half pound or so, its fighting qualities were far superior to those of coarse fish which are rather lethargic and sluggish in comparison. George was soon back in the water casting with renewed enthusiasm at the many fish rising in front of him, leaving me to empty my waders and wring out as much water as possible from two pairs of socks. It was not a very pleasant experience returning my warm, dry feet into cold, damp socks and then into waders which had retained a fair proportion of the water. One lesson I learnt from this episode was to mark the bank clearly at the point of entry by some stone, branch, extra-large tussock of grass or the relative position of a tree, before wading into any river or reservoir.

Jack, Cyril and Fred appeared as usual, Fred pausing to pass the time of day while Jack and Cyril wandered on, casting at fish as they went until they disappeared from view. He was thrilled to hear that I had landed my first fish and asked about the fly I had used and which part of the river it had been taken from. He remained near me for some time, which enabled me to watch his casting technique, and through our conversation I was able to learn much from his long experience of fishing the Derwent. He then moved on, stopping to have a few words with George and Arnie; it was the start of a long friendship between the four of us which continues to this day, although our visits to the Derwent are now very infrequent.

During those early years Fred never missed a Saturday. He could always be easily recognised plodding up or down the river by the way he carried his rod, and by the way his bag was slung over his rounded and stooping shoulders. He never failed to stop and pass on useful bits of information on where good fish were rising or what fly he had taken a fish on. One of his pet phrases when things were difficult, as they often were, was 'Plenty of fish rising, but I don't know the answer'. This phrase still springs to my mind whenever the fish are proving difficult to catch.

Over the last twenty years, I have read numerous books on fly fishing and talked with many people on the subject, but I consider that my success as a game fisherman is largely due to knowledge gleaned from Fred in those first few years. He was a loner by nature, and I have seen him retreat rapidly when other anglers have come into view rather than have any conversation with them, so it gave me great pleasure that he was prepared to spend so much time with George, Arnie and myself. I could not help feeling that our attitude to the sport, the river and its surroundings, and the way we conducted ourselves, must be quite acceptable if we were gaining the respect of Fred, whom we had come to regard as a gentleman, a fisherman and a true sportsman.

CHAPTER TEN

After my first success it was some weeks before the Derwent surrendered another fish, despite the long hours we spent there and our hard endeavours. We began to explore new areas of river rather than remain riveted to our favourite places. George disappeared in his characteristic manner, but Arnie and I made our way upstream until we reached a section where a stream joins the main river from somewhere high up in the hills. The river is particularly wide at this point and many fish were rising amongst the weeds which grew in abundance close to each bank. 'We can both fish here,' I said to Arnie. He agreed and elected to stay on the near bank.

Access was made relatively easy by dropping into the shallow stream and it was not many minutes before we were on our respective sides of the river; although we were just about level with each other we were yards apart. As on so many previous occasions, our artificial flies floated down over the places where fish were repeatedly rising, only to be ignored. Very occasionally a half-hearted swirl appeared underneath, which usually meant changing the fly pattern on the assumption that the one we had just presented was not quite right. After one of many such changes, an excited shout from Arnie told me that he was into a fish. I could see his rod bending as it reacted to the strain. Quickly I retrieved my line and, with my landing net unclipped and ready, made my way across to offer assistance. I was only halfway there when the fish was in Arnie's net. Close inspection showed it to be a very small grayling, but the delight on Arnie's face reflected his pride and sense of achievement at catching his first fish on the fly.

'This calls for a pipe of tobacco,' he said excitedly after he had returned the fish to the water and watched its speedy disappearance. Once more I made my way across the river leaving him semi-recumbent on the bank, with a very self-satisfied expression on his face, inhaling and then slowly, contentedly exhaling volumes of smoke which he had drawn from his pipe.

Some time later, when he had finished with his pipe, which was probably by now either empty or too hot to handle, and I had recorded my second fish, he began fishing again. He was soon into his second fish and, in response to my offers of help, assured me that everything was under control. Judging by the way the rod was bending it certainly looked a much larger fish than the one which had brought him so much pleasure earlier on. Arnie had a long battle with it, playing it as it used the river and the weeds in an effort to escape. At last I could see its head above the water, which was an indication that the fight was almost over. Arnie landed it expertly, crouching elegantly, one hand holding his net poised in the water while he slowly led the now tired fish into it with the other, which was holding the rod high above the river.

He remained in the river while he removed the hook from what appeared to be a very good trout. He had found that by placing the handle of the rod in his coat pocket and holding the rod higher up with the crook of his arm, his hand became free to remove the fish from the net. Once this had been accomplished he released the net, leaving it suspended in the water by the elastic while he used this hand to remove the hook. Very clever, I thought, as I watched the operation with interest, realising how many trips to the bank it would save. He held up the fish to give me a clearer view of it, asking me whether I considered it large enough for the frying pan. The words 'frying pan' must have really upset the fish because as soon as they were uttered it gave a wriggle, slid out of Arnie's hand like a piece of wet soap and shot back into the river — which immediately altered my opinion about the merits of removing a fly while remaining in the water.

Arnie prodded and probed amongst the weeds with his net in a desperate attempt to recapture the fish, but to no avail. His smiles of pleasure changed to a look of distinct unhappiness as thoughts of a fresh trout sizzling in the pan, or a visual record of such a fine fish, disappeared before his very eyes. He did, however, see the funny side later when I described to George what had happened. 'At least you've caught fish, which is more than I have,' was George's comment as he began to tell us about his own day, which was like so many others: plenty of fish to cast at but not a single fish interested in his fly.

As usual, Syd's eyes began to water and his shoulders to shake with laughter when we related the story of 'Arnie's slippery fish' over a pint at the Chequers. In fact, after the initial disappointment, the more the story was told the funnier it became. That and other similar cruelties of the hour fade as the years go by and the more amusing side of such events and incidents becomes paramount. We did not talk about the discomforts of being cold, wet and miserable, the times we spent searching the river when few fish were rising or the frustrations of losing a fish as Arnie had done on this occasion. We did, however, reminisce repeatedly about the lighter side of our experiences, and found it much easier to recall such incidents as the maggots in the boot at Ely than a day when it was impossible to cast due to a howling gale.

I suppose if this were not true — and if every fish were caught and landed in perfect conditions and we could not accept disappointment or failure — fishing would be far too serious or predictable to be appreciated; I am sure I would not be enjoying the sport as I have done for nearly forty years. Some fishermen's sole aim is to catch fish and at any cost. They judge themselves and pride themselves on how many fish they have caught and how big they were. It saddens me when I hear such people, to think how much fun and pleasure from natural and unnatural events must be wasted, if the only criterion for their enjoyment of fishing is to catch as many fish as possible, as big as possible and no doubt as quickly as possible. I am very grateful that none of my fishing acquaintances or friends have ever fallen into this category.

* * *

October the sixteenth, which marks the end of the season for trout, arrived all too quickly, although even this had its compensations. The trees, bracken and fern began to change colour from their ageing summer green to the yellows, reds and browns of autumn. The rays of the sun penetrating the early morning mist made the trees stand out like red and orange beacons. The tracks of cattle could easily be seen where they had broken the cobwebs or disturbed the dew, leaving dark green meanderings through a silver sheen. The plump water voles were busy making last-minute preparations for weeks of hibernation, and the mallards and moorhens seemed quietly contented, having successfully raised their young. Fewer fish were showing as the fly hatch became more and more restricted and the breeding time for the trout approached. Even the river appeared quiet and subdued as it wandered serenely through fields and woods and seemed pleased to be resting after weeks of activity.

The end of the trout season did not mean the end of our fishing on the Derwent, since it held numerous grayling. The grayling season corresponds with that of the coarse fishing season, which runs from June the sixteenth until March the sixteenth, the commencement of the new trout season; so our newly acquired tickets provided fishing in one form or another for the whole year.

In order to fish for grayling we had to revert to our coarse fishing tackle which had not seen the light of day since our excursion to Boroughbridge. Instead of fishing the fly on the surface we once again used the maggot or occasionally the worm for our bait which was fished underneath. I found it rather strange sitting on my basket, relatively inactive, watching the float for signs of a hungry fish, after the weeks of wading and stalking visibly feeding fish.

Fred once again proved to be most helpful, suggesting likely areas for grayling which he told us tended to shoal in the back eddies and deep pools, especially in heavy water after rain. We had incredible sport during those winter weeks, sometimes catching between ten and twenty fish, many of which were upwards of a pound in weight. George was particularly thrilled on these occasions and rapturised at great length about the sport such a river provided compared with the small and relatively few inedible fish we had caught in the past, except for the few days we had spent at Borough-bridge. George had yet to experience the thrill of catching a surface-feeding fish on the fly and was unable to make a comparison between the two. Arnie and I could, and although we enjoyed the winter's sport, the fresh air and attendant social activities, we both had a yearning for March and the exciting prospects of more fly fishing.

After one very successful day, we decided to present Bert, our landlord at the Chequers, with six of our largest fish. Syd had often mentioned the excellent eating qualities of the grayling which he had caught as a temporary diversion while fishing for salmon on the River Test in Hampshire. Bert had an annoying habit of sarcastically singing 'The Fishermen of England' as soon as we arrived, followed by the usual banal comments suggesting that the only thing we had caught all day was a cold. We could tell, to within one or two, how many people were inside by how loudly he sang or commented in a bid to become the centre of attention.

'There must be a few in tonight,' I said to Arnie and

George as Bert heartily and ostentatiously performed his aria and made his predictable comment when we came through the door. Presenting Bert with the fish would quieten him once and for all, and relieve us and the locals of this repetitious and monotonous greeting, we thought, after we had suppressed our urge to stop the utterances with a strategically placed cold, wet fish.

Bert obliged without question when I asked him if I could borrow a large tray. I slipped out to the car and fetched the fish, arranging them neatly on the tray before walking back through the bar in waiter style and placing them on one of the tables.

'There you are, Bert, enjoy those,' I said.

Bert was unusually and temporarily speechless for a while when he looked at the tray and its contents of six fresh, gleaming, silver-blue fish, all identical in size. The peace did not last for very long. Before we had taken the top off a pint, Bert was parading the fish through the pub, showing them off to everyone in his own inimitable way. Although we were sitting in our usual places in the bar, we could easily hear him in the front room directing the attention of the unsuspecting customers to the fish.

'Just look at these,' he ordered. 'What do you think of these? Aren't they beautiful?' Returning to our room, he began a repeat performance, completely ignoring anyone who needed serving. He duly showed everyone in our room before placing the fish on the table in front of us, asking us where and how they had been caught and estimating their weight, until he reluctantly realised that he was required to do some work at the bar.

All of a sudden I was horrified to see a maggot wriggling along the bottom of the tray between two of the fish. A closer inspection revealed several more, one even crawling out of the mouth of one of the fish. I quickly took hold of the tray while I informed Bert that the heat of the room was drying out the fish and that before he put them in the fridge, which I suggested would be the best place for them, I would wash them down for him. I was already halfway to the wash basin in the Gents' toilet when Bert began assuring me that he would see to them, and I was inside with the door shut before he had finished the sentence. I poured gallons of water into the stomachs of the fish to wash out the undigested maggots, and it was quite some time before I was satisfied that any remaining maggots were safely in the fishes' digestive systems.

'What was that all about?' asked Arnie after Bert had left for the kitchen, obviously quite unaware of what had happened. I explained about the undigested maggots and what I had done to remedy the situation. Needless to say they were both very pleased that they had not noticed anything untoward and grateful that a very embarrassing moment had been avoided.

'If Bert had seen that,' exclaimed George, 'we would never have heard the last of it and it would have been the major topic of conversation for the next twelve months.'

'More like twelve years!' muttered Arnie dryly, raising his glass to me as a sign of appreciation.

CHAPTER ELEVEN

March finally arrived and we could look forward to our first full season after the delayed beginning of the year before. Arnie and I searched the river with our fly rods during those cool days, looking for the first tell-tale dimples created by surface-feeding fish, while George preferred to carry on fishing for grayling until one or two fish began to rise during a limited fly hatch, which usually occurred some time during the afternoon. He would then change over and fish the fly for a while, before returning to his basket and one of his favourite grayling holes as soon as he thought most of the activity was over. He was not quite so enthusiastic or as dedicated to the fly as Arnie and I had become, although I could not help thinking that it would only take one fish caught on fly to change his attitude.

The days and the water began to warm up, with a resultant increase in surface activity. The moorhens returned to the water, together with the mallards, and the banks became active with the to-ing and fro-ing of water voles, obviously refreshed after their long winter sleep. Flies began to hatch in larger numbers and for a longer period of time. The elderberry, for so long grey and lifeless, awoke with hints of green, followed by the hawthorn and eventually the alders which stood like guardsmen on the banks, providing welcome cover for the fishermen and sanctuary for flies and the many and varied birds. Swathes of light and dark green appeared in the grassy meadows after tractor-drawn harrows had teased out the old grass to encourage and make way for the new; the brown fields of winter barley, which had been

The River Derwent.

lying dormant, rapidly changed to carpets of shimmering green; and the well-orchestrated sounds of the birds claiming and defending their territory made a welcome change after the silence of the winter months.

Syd applied to join the Derby Railway Institute Fishing Club again after years of absence, so that he could participate in our activities, rather than listen to our enthusiastic accounts of the day's fishing over a pint later in the evening when we returned to the Chequers. Wim, another keen fisherman and domino player, also applied, although he had already had access to other rivers through his father who was a well-known and respected fisherman. I had known Wim for many years in my cricketing days, although we played for different teams, and it was only when he joined us on Friday nights that his passion for fishing began to emerge. Business commitments meant that he was away for weeks at a time, very often in the Far East, so that he missed many of our conversations; it was therefore only natural that his fishing experiences and interests were slow to reveal themselves, in comparison with those of Syd whom we met regularly. They were both accepted into the Club, but, like us during our first year, they had to wait until June before they could begin fishing, while we could fish the early season.

Even when the fish began rising freely during early May, they remained very difficult to catch, in spite of our increased skill and the confidence we had gained from the previous season. We began to differentiate between the numerous flies which hatched on the river. We could recognise the subtle difference between the lighter and darker olives and make comparisons between the size of these and the smaller gnats. Instead of merely seeing a fly on the surface, totally disregarding its size and colour, we tried to choose our patterns to match those we had observed. We could also recognise drag, which occurs when the fly line is moving more quickly than the current in which the fly is floating. After a few seconds the faster floating line would pull the fly along rather than leaving it to float naturally in the slower current, creating a wake which made even the most constantly rising fish dubious about its authenticity. Sometimes even the slightest innocuous-looking drag would completely stop a fish rising, which was very frustrating if time and effort had been spent in reaching what we thought was a favourable position from which to cast. In an effort to overcome this problem, I would spend time casting into likely-looking feeding places for trout and would carefully watch the fly to see if it was travelling at the same speed as the river, comparing it with the unattached bits and pieces which float on any river's surface. If drag did occur I would try to eradicate it by casting from different positions in the river, or would attempt to cast some slack line onto the water, giving the fly more time to float naturally before the current straightened out the line and the speed-boat effect became apparent. I enjoyed these practice sessions, and felt very satisfied with the knowledge I was gaining about the intricacies of fishing and the habits of the river.

Arnie, too, had a thirst for knowledge, taking time off from fishing to observe more intently what was happening on the river. Very often I would find him sitting on the bank, pipe in hand, earnestly watching the way a particular fish was feeding or keenly watching Fred to see how he attempted to deceive various fish. George, on the other hand, was more of a practical fisherman and was inclined to fish continuously, working on the theory that a fish would never be caught while his bait was out of the water, and that by the law of averages a fish was eventually going to fall to his fly. From what we could gather from the references he made or from the few occasions we were allowed to witness him fishing, observation of anything other than the immediate fish was strictly limited.

Nevertheless, in his own way he was totally absorbed in his efforts, to such a degree that very often he was completely unaware of our presence. We could hear him talking to himself while he fished. 'Steady, lad. Don't go too far,' as he edged further into the river and the water began to creep towards the top of his waders. He would chastise himself most severely when the line made a splash upon the water, or would congratulate himself on a good cast. He must have thought that the fish had a good command of the English language by the way he spoke to them. Sometimes quite politely with 'Come on, take that fly, it's beautiful,' but on other occasions a hint of frustration would creep in: 'Well, I don't know what you want. Do you want the box to choose your own?'

Arnie and I would listen to this for a while before one of us, in a deliberately loud voice, would shout from our concealed position, 'Morning, George!' which shattered his concentration and made him jump visibly. 'You silly buggers!' we could hear coming over the noise of the water as he made his way towards the bank. His first fish was something of an anti-climax: he calmly informed us of his success, in a very matter-of-fact manner, although inwardly, I am sure, he was as excited as we had been when we hooked and landed our first fish.

We continued to fish each Saturday with varying degrees of success. George, with increased confidence, began to catch one or two fish after his disappointing and unfruitful first few introductory months. As the weeks went by the flies began to hatch in great abundance and the increased activity of the fish became very obvious. The swallows had returned, heralding the beginning of summer and making demands on the prolific and lengthening fly hatch. It was noticeable how much softer and more mellow the water looked after the harsh, cold appearance of winter and early spring.

Although we were enjoying our fishing, we were eagerly awaiting the Mayfly hatch which occurs at the end of May or beginning of June. Many accounts of fishing the Mayfly have been published in books and magazines, where it is usually referred to as 'Duffers' fortnight', when trout rise with gay abandon and supposedly give themselves up to the least experienced fisherman. Fred confirmed that the Mayfly hatch was indeed good on the Derwent and that many of the larger trout only surface-feed during this particular time, preferring to feed on the bottom for the rest of the year.

We did not know what to expect. We had not even seen a real Mayfly. The previous year, due to our mid-June beginning to the season, we had begun our fishing after the hatch had finished.

Sure enough, on the last Saturday in May it all began. It was about mid-morning when I first noticed, at a distance, what appeared to be leaves floating on the river, until ripples radiating from several of them made me realise that they were flies agitating and stretching their wings in a prelude to their maiden flight. I was amazed at their sheer size. The largest flies I had experienced were the early and late season olives, which were only some half an inch long. These were at least two inches long from the head to the end of the abdomen and twice as long if the length of the three tails protruding from the end was taken into account. The height of the wings was about two inches, so it was hardly surprising that I had mistaken them for leaves after a casual glance. I was hypnotised by the ethereal way they rose from the water, slowly, gently and silently beating their gossamer wings.

Very carefully I lifted one from the water and placed it on the back of my hand, where a close inspection revealed what must be one of the most beautiful species in the insect world, and certainly one of the most beautiful creatures on our rivers. The body is divided into about eight segments, each one beginning a pale yellow before gradually changing to a dark greeny brown before the contrasting yellow of the next segment begins. The upright wings are a delicate latticework, fragile, transparent and intricate, resembling a miniature but irregular spider's web, with a soft blue-grey tinge of colour. The three tails extending from the abdomen are dark brown and held apart as if proud to be an integral part of such a

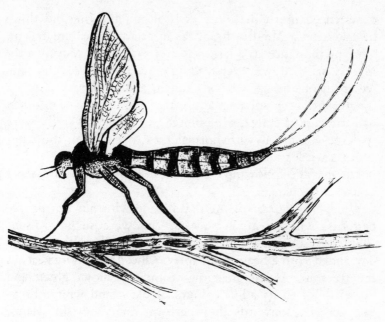

THE MAYFLY

spectacular life form. Why, I wondered, was the Mayfly allowed only hours or two days at most to live, once it had emerged from its two years on the river bed? Surely such a delight deserved more than that!

Although I was preoccupied with the sight of the Mayfly, it did occur to me, while I was wandering up the river, that although many fish were rising, the now easily recognisable Mayfly were being ignored. They were left to float down the river unmolested, before taking off and gracefully flying to settle on some convenient tree, unless the ever-hungry swallows, swifts or housemartins brought their lives to an abrupt end. It appeared that the trout preferred other flies for their diet, which was a complete contradiction of the many reports of trouts' gluttony during Mayfly time.

During our mid-day refreshments, we discussed what was happening before our very eyes. George and Arnie had experienced much the same as I, although Arnie did think he had seen a Mayfly disappear in a large swirl created by what he thought was a larger-than-average fish. Mayfly after Mayfly sailed down over feeding trout throughout the time we spent on the bank having lunch, and not one was taken by a trout. Fred solved the mystery for us when he joined us for a cup of coffee. He pointed out that the Mayfly were so large compared with normal flies that it took the trout about a week to get used to them before they began feeding on them. The following week, he told us, we would see a remarkable change.

We spent the rest of the day fishing with our normal fly patterns, without much success, and were slightly disenchanted by our first experience of the Mayfly, although the day ended with a beautiful display. Once the Mayfly reaches the trees it moults, changing from its yellow, green and brown hues to its adult colours of black and white. From early evening onwards they perform their courtship dance by the side of the river. Thousands are on the wing, forming what look like misty clouds surrounding the trees. They suddenly rise three or four feet with their tails spread and then drop like stones before rising again. This ritual is incessant and spectacular and lasts well into the evening, before the females leave to lay their eggs in the river by depositing them on the water, from where they will sink to the bottom and remain lying in the gravel beds, before rising up to give another unrehearsed display. Late evening is a sharp contrast to the morning, as spent and dying Mayflies litter the surface and are carried away to a watery grave.

As Fred had promised, the following Saturday did produce a remarkable change. The river seemed particularly active as we surveyed the scene from the car park by the water's edge. Instead of the usual swirls or gentle dimples spotting the surface, exaggerated splashes were occurring as far as the eye could see. 'This is it,' said George as he rapidly unloaded the boot and then made feverish attempts at tackling up. He was more than a little annoyed when he noticed that he had done Arnie's trick and that his line had bypassed one of the rod rings, which meant removing the fly and beginning all over again. His anxiety also showed when his heavily socked foot yet again temporarily refused to reach the bottom of his waders. Nevertheless, after a while all was ready and we were off, each with an artificial Mayfly on the end of our line. George did his by now customary disappearing act up the river, while Arnie methodically lit his pipe and began to observe what was happening. I stayed with him for a while before making my way downstream to some fast, well-weeded water which had become one of my favourite spots. A densely wooded hillside sloped down towards me, opening out onto a steep, grassy area by the river. The bank was high and lined with trees which shaded half the water. In the early months of summer wild flowers grew in the grass, providing a sea of colour — the delicate pink of soapwort, the stark

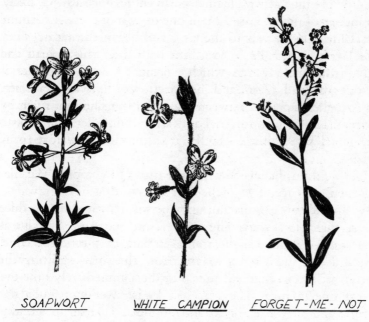

SOAPWORT   WHITE CAMPION   FORGET-ME-NOT

white of campions and the pastel blue clumps of the familiar forget-me-nots — a wonderful example of one of nature's gardens.

I paused several times on the way down to watch the path of a Mayfly, to see how far it floated before being frantically devoured by some trout, or to watch it take off and make for the safety of the trees after running the gauntlet of the swallows. Some would take off just a foot or so in front of where a trout was feeding, only to be plucked from the air at an alarming speed. I could not help feeling how unjust it all seemed: it had taken two years for the Mayfly to change from an egg to a fly, and then within seconds many were doomed to be food for fish or bird.

I was very pleased to see that several trout were rising in the channels among the weed beds when I finally arrived at the place where I intended to begin fishing. Sure enough, I could clearly see them taking the Mayfly, which were following the narrow channels in an endless procession. Only a matter of time before I catch one or two of these, I thought as I made my way into the river and began casting over the first fish. Normally it was difficult to see which particular fly, from the varieties which were hatching, an individual trout was feeding on, and the selection of fly was very often a speculative choice between several of our imitations. There would be no need for trial and error today, I thought, as I watched my artificial Mayfly and confidently waited for a fish to take it.

I could not believe it when the first fish completely disregarded it. I carefully watched for signs of drag as my artificial fly floated towards me amongst the weeds, checking to make sure that it was travelling at the same speed as the natural flies. All appeared to be well, yet time after time the trout would crazily snatch a Mayfly from the surface directly in front of my fly, ignore mine and then immediately take the next one in turn. The next fish I cast over was much the same and so was the next and the next. I began to wonder

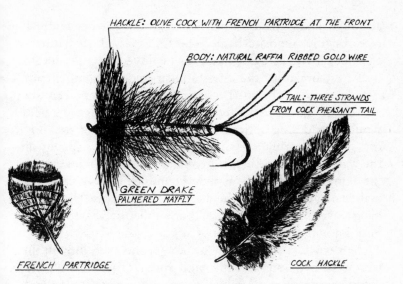

HACKLE: OLIVE COCK WITH FRENCH PARTRIDGE AT THE FRONT

BODY: NATURAL RAFFIA RIBBED GOLD WIRE

TAIL: THREE STRANDS FROM COCK PHEASANT TAIL

GREEN DRAKE PALMERED MAYFLY

FRENCH PARTRIDGE

COCK HACKLE

what was wrong. The artificial fly I had selected was a 'Green Drake' and looked a perfect imitation of the real thing both in size and colour.

It was becoming increasingly infuriating as the fish greedily snapped up every Mayfly within reasonable reach, making the water boil but leaving my fly dancing on the waves it had created. Very occasionally one would swirl under my fly, appearing to leave it at the very last second, knowing it to be false. So much for 'Duffers' Fortnight', I thought as I made my way back to the car to meet Arnie and George. They were already there when I arrived, in deep conversation with Fred and, judging from their remarks, they, too, had had a particularly disappointing morning. Philosophically Fred remarked that the Derwent fish were the most educated fish in England and that the fishing would probably improve during the evening when the sun was past its height. Despite the lack of reward from our morning's efforts, after a hurried lunch the constantly rising fish compelled us to return to meet the challenge once again.

The afternoon proved to be much the same as the morning,

although I did manage one nice trout taken from under the trees on the opposite bank. The time passed very quickly, and not only in actual fishing, for I enjoyed several interludes just contemplating the environment and watching nature's dramas unfold. The antics of the water voles were a constant source of amusement and very difficult to ignore. They would spend long periods preening themselves or basking in the sun, appearing to fall asleep and promptly falling into the water from some ledge. I could see — or did I imagine? — the expression of shock as they scrambled back to their original vantage point on the bank, wiping water from their bleary eyes. They would take it upon themselves, for reasons best known to water voles, to cross the river where the current was at its strongest, losing ground even though their legs were paddling at whirlwind speed. Their faces wore a distinct expression of achievement and a certain amount of relief when they reached the opposite bank. The wagtails and chaffinches would try to emulate the swallows in feeding on the fly but appeared very pedestrian by comparison, as they hovered over the water and made clumsy attempts at catching lunch or tea before returning to the comparative safety of bush or tree.

As the shadows lengthened, more and more fish began to rise. I noticed this particularly in the bays which were slightly away from the main stream. The sound of splashes and crashes echoed in those well-sheltered spots as fish vigorously pursued their prey leaving waves radiating from their tell-tale lies. I decided to change my 'Green Drake' Mayfly to a black and white one which was similar to the adult flies I had seen dancing by the trees the week before. I entered the water shaking with excitement. There were so many fish rising that I found it increasingly difficult to concentrate on one at a time. Just as I had fixed my sights and attentions on one fish in particular, another would loop over and crash back into the water just to the right, and then another just behind, which distracted me from the original fish. Keep calm, I thought to myself, and slow down. This was good advice but difficult to achieve with heart pounding, pulse racing and constantly rising fish catching my eye from all directions.

Eventually I cast over a fish which was rising quite freely close to the bank in one of the bays. I watched the fly float down and disappear in a swirl, the ferocity of which I had never experienced before: the fish had taken the fly and expelled it again before I had struck to set the hook, so slow were my reactions. I was a little more prepared for the next fish. Down the fly came and disappeared. I struck. There was a thump as the hook made contact with the fish — and then nothing. The fish was gone and so was the fly. This happened again with the next fish. The intensity of the take was so great that the fine nylon in the large eye of the hook was breaking on impact. I was reluctant to leave the river, but the only thing to do was to change the leader. I had been fishing with nylon of two and a half pound strength, which I needed to increase to at least four pounds. It seemed hours before I was back in the water. I had tried to undo the new leader in far too much haste, which resulted in a bunch of nylon looking more like a construction any bird would have been proud of. I uncoiled another leader and attached it to the fly line and tied onto it my third Mayfly, which felt much more secure on the thicker four-pound nylon.

Once more I was in position behind the fish and once more carefully watching the fly gracefully floating down the river amongst the many natural ones, until it disappeared in a swirl. I hooked the fish with a quick lift of the rod. This time I maintained contact with the fish as it darted about unpredictably in an effort to shed the hook, and then I had him safely in the net. I hooked and landed three more fish before Arnie arrived, followed shortly afterwards by George. They, too, had caught fish but had suffered in much the same way as I had, losing several good fish before they changed to a stronger leader. We agreed, however, that

107

fishing the Mayfly had, after all, lived up to its reputation as one of the most exciting times on the river; although later, over a quiet pint, we decided that the term 'Duffers' Fortnight' was somewhat inaccurate, at least according to our experience.

* * *

It was difficult, during the next few days, to forget the experience. Visions of the river with all those flies hatching and so many fish rising appeared time after time in my subconscious and tormented me so much that I decided to visit the river again, straight from work on the following Wednesday evening. The day passed maddeningly slowly, but at last the time came to set off. I had thought that it would take less time than usual to reach the river, since my place of work was several miles closer than my home was. In fact the journey seemed endless. I became more and more convinced that every traffic light, slow-moving lorry or roadworks was deliberately set to hinder rapid progress.

Eventually I was changed, tackled up and by the river, very grateful to be away from the noise and fumes of so-called civilisation. I was happy and contented at the prospect of having nature as a companion for the evening, but still eager to be down at my favourite stretch of river. I hurried along the bank, panting in my haste, perspiration forming on my brow and attracting numerous flies which were usually content to remain near the cowpats adorning the adjacent fields. I was contemplating how good the prospects were looking with the Mayflies dancing by the trees in their thousands, when a voice coming from the direction of the trees startled me and stopped me abruptly in my tracks.

'Lovely evening and a good fly hatch.' I could hear, although I could not see where the voice was coming from.

'Yes,' I said, peering round and trying to place the source of the voice.

'Some lovely fish rising here,' he went on, which attracted my gaze to an old man who was crouching behind a tree and was pretty well obscured by the tall grasses.

'Good,' I said, 'hope you catch them.' And I moved on very quickly, not wishing to prolong the time before I could begin fishing. What is he doing there? I thought to myself as I strode off. It was an impossible place to fish, surrounded by so many trees, high banks and tall grasses, a place which, by my reckoning, did not warrant a second glance.

I was soon fishing with limited success. The fish were still very active but more reluctant to take the fly than they had been the previous Saturday evening. Progression upstream eventually brought me back to the trees. With so much to do and so much happening, I had temporarily forgotten about my earlier encounter, until the same voice said, 'Just caught another.' I looked in disbelief as the old man struggled up the bank with a huge fish in his net which must have weighed some two pounds. He calmly knocked the fish on the head with his priest and retrieved his fly from its mouth. Then he parted the grass and laid the fish alongside another one of similar size.

'That'll do me,' he said. 'A nice brace.'

'Beautiful!' I gasped. I had not even realised that fish in the Derwent grew to that sort of size. 'How did you cast out to catch those?'

'Son,' he said, 'providing you are patient, quiet and crafty there is no need to cast a long line here. There is no need to wade the river disturbing the fish, either. Two yards of line flicked round the trees is quite sufficient. Besides, the exertion of wading and casting a long line is too much for me now.'

Suddenly I noticed his rod as he carefully placed it on the bank out of harm's way. It had a solid greenheart butt with brass fittings and a greenheart top piece. It was old Mr Hendy who had given me the incentive to begin fishing, and now here was another dear old gentleman who had politely told me how it was done. I had much to think about as I walked pensively back to the car.

I felt very humble driving home, somewhat embarrassed and more than a little annoyed at what had happened. I knew it all, or so I thought, to such an extent that I had questioned why the old man was fishing in the trees, in a place which I considered quite inappropriate. Who was I to judge, with my limited experience and knowledge, compared to his? Why had I not stopped to watch him and gain experience from his craft and guile instead of rushing off in such an ignorant and inconsiderate manner? Even passing the time of day with him had seemed an intrusion and an imposition. Yes, I had progressed from those early days on the Derwent at Duffield. Yes, I could cast a reasonable line, fairly accurately after much practice. Yes, I could detect drag and compensate for it, and I knew more about flies and their imitations. But when it came down to it, I still had much to learn.

CHAPTER TWELVE

I described my visit to the Derwent and my encounter with the old man to Arnie and George at the Chequers on the Friday evening, before our customary game of dominoes. This made them even more eager to be on the way to the river the following day, although I could not help feeling that they were more impressed with the size of the fish than with the way they had been caught. The fact that the Mayfly were still hatching in abundance and that trout were still feeding on them seemed far more important to them than learning from probably years of experience of where and how large fish could be caught. This left me wondering whether I should have told them at all; perhaps one had to see for oneself to appreciate it fully.

We arrived at the Derwent very early the following morning. The river received its usual inspection to make sure that all was well, and we assembled our tackle with the usual bustle and sense of purpose. George was soon disappearing into the distance, while Arnie and I were still packing our normal clothes and shoes into the boot.

As I wandered off downstream, leaving Arnie to light his pipe, I could not help noticing how much more leisurely my pace had become. I made strenuous efforts to observe the river from between the trees. I began to climb down the banks and through the trees and low branches, sometimes ending up precariously balanced with one foot on the bank and the other on the tree roots, in order to get a glimpse of places which I had never seen before. Some were obviously not favourite feeding grounds for fish, but in others I could see fish rising, although I found it impossible to reach them: either the high banks or low branches restricted the back-cast far too much, or else there was no secure foothold from which to cast at all. Nevertheless, I found it interesting sitting among the foliage watching fish rise at such close quarters, wondering if they realised that they were in little danger of ever being presented with an artificial offering.

After a while I decided to walk down the river and begin making my way upstream from a point which would bring me back to the car in time for lunch. It was also the only effective way to fish, since all fish face upstream and have to be approached from behind. I had noticed on my way down, that when I appeared from between the trees, the fish immediately downstream of me would stop rising, obviously having seen me, while those rising immediately above showed no alarm and were completely unaware of my presence.

Progress upstream was very slow and completely different from the way I had fished before. Instead of bypassing the trees on my side of the river I was in amongst them, peering round trunks from a crouched or kneeling position; I even found myself hanging on to a trunk with one arm and leaning out over the bank to gain a clear view of the river. From some of these positions I could see trout rising sometimes only feet in front of me and inches away from the bank. The difficulty was actually to cast a fly over them. Normally I would be standing upright in the river casting twenty or so yards of line overhead, unrestricted and with complete freedom of movement. Now I was hampered not only by the trees and bank but by lack of movement from my own awkward position. It was impossible to raise the rod verti-cally, let alone cast. As I focused on a beautiful trout rising steadily just in front of me, how I wished I had watched the previous Wednesday. I could see it as it leisurely broke the surface sipping in a Mayfly, in complete contrast to the way fish were feeding in the more open stretches. For a second or two I could see its large dorsal fin hovering above the water before it disappeared as the trout returned to its lie. How many of these sipping rises must I have missed in my obsession to be where fish were noisily and more obviously rising.

It must be possible to cast over the fish, I thought. After all, I had seen those beautiful trout caught by the old man from a similar position only a few days ago. I tested the depth of the river by gently lowering one leg into the water and, although it looked deep, my foot came to rest on what felt like a stone before the water came to the top of my waders. It was difficult to persuade the other leg to follow from its kneeling position on the bank. One false move would frighten the trout, which concerned me more than any thoughts for my own safety. The water appeared black in the shade of the trees, which made it impossible for me to see the bottom and what I was standing on. After a while I felt reasonably secure with both feet in the river and just away from the bank. All this time I never once took my eyes from that rising fish, making sure that my ungainly movements had not frightened him away. I was only a foot or so away from the trees, so a back-cast was impossible.

After weighing up the situation, I decided that the only way to cast up to the fish was to point my arm and rod out over the river and let it follow a path sideways and parallel to the bank. I found that casting horizontally rather than vertically in such a restricted way gave me much less power in my wrist and forearm, which upset my rhythm. It was difficult to adapt to this new technique even with such a short line; I lost distance and accuracy and the fly repeatedly caught the water. Rather than cast over the fish immediately I practised for a while, making sure that any splash from a poor cast was well away from the fish which was still rising freely.

Eventually I felt confident enough to attempt my first cast over the quarry. Gradually I increased the length of line until I felt it was long enough for the fly to reach the fish. My final back-cast stopped with a sudden jerk and the sound of rustling in the trees. I followed the line back until I could see it attached to one of the branches which firmly held the fly. I was more than a little annoyed at having to climb out of the water to release the fly before carefully and painstakingly returning to my previous position. The exertions of climbing, bending and standing in the water on one leg for a while, to allow the ripples to subside before carefully replacing the remaining leg, made my limbs ache and perspiration was running from my forehead and down the small of my back. The perspiration on my face attracted numerous flies of the household variety which buzzed round annoyingly and settled either on my nose or just underneath my eyes. It was difficult to get rid of them with both hands engaged in manipulating the rod and line; besides, swatting them would have created a disturbance which was the very thing I was trying to avoid. My only defence was to try to blow them away with jets of air exhaled upwards alternately from each corner of my mouth, like a steam train hissing when it was under pressure leaving a station.

Once again I sent my line arching forwards towards the fish which was still head and tailing just in front of me. One last back-cast and a little more line released would give me enough length of line on the forward cast to land the fly just above the trout. The result was a complete disaster. Instead of the line straightening and the fly alighting gently on the river, it concertinaed, landing in a heap just where the fish was rising. An enormous swirl, followed by the tell-tale lack of activity at the place where the fish had been rising, which I had been watching so intently and for so long, told me that the fish was gone. How had the old man done it without wading? I began to wonder, looking at the trees over-hanging the water's edge. I was hot, breathless and my legs ached with standing precariously balanced in the water, while he had looked so cool, calm and collected and had made it sound so easy. I could not help feeling that I had frightened away

114

a larger than average fish through my lack of skill and technique, although I felt reasonably satisfied with myself for at least attempting to fish from such a position.

I could see more fish rising further up the river, so all was not lost. To avoid climbing out I thought I would try to reach the next fish by wading upstream. When my testing foot could not make contact with the river bed I made use of the tree roots, But I had to make frequent stops when my line became entangled in the branches. I nearly came to grief bypassing a tree where the river was very deep. Only a fool would try this method of progress, I thought, as I hung suspended over the water, with a foot either side of the tree which I was embracing in an effort to avoid disaster. As I placed my foot and arm round the tree the trout bag, which was hanging from my shoulder, became trapped between me, the tree and my other arm, making it impossible to move. Hoping the roots would not give way, I made frantic undulating movements to free the offending bag, which I eventually managed after much effort; only when I had circumnavigated the tree did I begin to wonder what this spectacle must have looked like viewed from the opposite bank.

I had to approach the next fish in much the same way as the first, with my rod extended out over the water and trying to persuade the line to trace a path parallel to the bank. If my arm went only slightly past the point where it was at right angles to the bank, the line would go too far round and the fly would attach itself to some tree or to the grass on the bank. Occasionally a quick tug would release the fly, but more often than not it would remain firmly attached, secured with a perfectly formed half-hitch to a branch or piece of grass or held firm by the barb of the hook which was embedded in the bark of a very innocent-looking trunk.

A quick glance at my watch told me that it was some fifteen minutes past the time we had arranged for lunch. I must have spent just over three hours in the trees, much of this being taken up in trying to gain a satisfactory position

115

from which to cast or in retrieving the fly from some obstacle or other. I suddenly realised that in that time I had not managed to cast properly over one fish, but I was quietly well satisfied with my efforts and felt that I was learning a great deal.

'Where the hell have you been?' asked George and Arnie who were already sitting by the car when I arrived some minutes later.

'Sorry I'm late,' I replied, 'but I didn't realise what time it was.'

'What have you been doing?' they enquired rather quizzically.

'Why?' I asked. It was only when they pointed it out to me that I realised I was filthy! My coat was green with moss from the trees; my waders were scratched and etched from kneeling or climbing up and down the banks or from the rough treatment they had received from inconsiderately positioned trees; my hands were impregnated with dust and grime from the branches and soil from the bank, some of which, judging from George's comments, must have been deposited on my face whilst wiping away perspiration.

'Some lovely fish down there,' I informed them, as a piece of twig fell from my hair and onto my sandwiches, 'and how have you got on?'

'Not too bad,' came the reply, which seemed to fade into the distance as thoughts of the fish located by the trees and on our side of the river painted vivid pictures in my mind.

When I arrived back at the point where I had left the river, curiosity compelled me to go further down to see if the first fish I had spotted was rising again. Would he have overcome the frightening ordeal of the morning? I wondered, as I walked out into the field to avoid detection from the river. Once more in position, much to my delight I could see the fin and part of a broad back every few seconds as the fish constantly fed, obviously fully recovered from the morning's fright.

'Compose yourself,' my subconscious kept telling me as I slipped into the water. It was much easier this time, for the experience I had gained in the morning told me that I was quite safe: the water was less than wader deep and the bed reasonably secure.

The break for lunch and my thoughts about casting horizontally must have had quite an effect. I found it much easier and less of an effort now, with the line moving far more freely up and down the river, taking the fly away from the snags on the bank and keeping it well above the water. My very first attempt at presenting the fly accurately just above the fish was very successful, and before I could finish congratulating myself the fish lifted and leisurely took the fly. I tightened and felt the fish. His response was quick and immediate. Within seconds he was out into the river, speeding downstream past me as he made for the safety of the roots. The branches which surrounded me made it awkward to lift the rod to take some of the strain and try to control the fish. I could not turn quickly while standing amongst the stones, which left the fish very much in command. I retrieved line until it went taut and formed a straight line between the rod tip and the roots below. As I half-expected, there was no movement; it confirmed my worst suspicions. He had taken advantage of too much freedom and had shed the hook, leaving it neatly embedded in the roots below me. How a fish can shed a hook so quickly and so easily with the aid of such obstacles I shall never know. I wondered how large he was and would have liked to know, but I graciously conceded that he had won this particular battle and nodded respectfully towards the place where he had been lying. At least I had gained a position close to him and managed to deceive him into taking my fly, but in the end he had shown me that he knew far more about that part of the river than I did. I sat for a while watching the river, which was quiet now after my brief but dramatic encounter, and watching the trees and bushes which appeared to be secretly guarding this and other tales which they would never, ever tell.

Continuing my walk up the river, it soon became apparent that the feeding habits of the fish varied greatly. Those in the open water were very noisy and obvious as they splashed about, compared with the unobtrusive small dimple and sedate rise of the fish which were close to the banks. It almost appeared as though the larger fish were lying in the cover of the banks and trees where they felt they could feed in comparative safety, leaving the smaller fish to take what they could from the more open water. This was confirmed to some extent while I was watching a pool, after I had left my position in the trees. Once my eyes had become accustomed to the bright sunlight I could see the flashes as the fish fed in the shallow pool. Moving closer, with the sun penetrating the water I could see several small grayling silhouetted against the gravel, jockeying for position before darting to the surface at great speed to devour a fly.

This should be easy and a pleasant respite, I thought, as I crept up behind them in the middle of the river, and something of a relief to be casting quite freely again after the confines of overhanging branches and tall grassy banks. The fly drifted down time and time again over those fish without any interest being shown on their part, although they were still rising with monotonous regularity to the steady stream of Mayflies. The fish in the vicinity of the trees had taken the fly readily, which brought me to the conclusion that the shadow or the visibility of the line in the bright sunshine must be having an adverse effect so that the fish could distinguish between my artificial fly and the real thing.

Leaving these fish, I made my way up the river, feeling somewhat defeated although not too despondent when I considered what I had achieved up to that point. The river turned to my left, making it possible to see both banks despite the foliage which grew in great profusion on either side. Fish were ringing the surface as far as my eye could

The River Derwent.

see, but the effects of the exertions of the morning and the heat of the afternoon compelled me to sit for a while. It was a pleasant interlude as I watched the fish and the birds feeding or listened to the cows grazing in the fields. I could hear the grass being torn up and the sound of numerous sets of teeth grinding it to pulp. The noises were growing louder and louder, and I wondered how near they would dare to come as with great difficulty I suppressed my natural desire to turn and see how far they had progressed. I could hear them breathing, snorting and sniffing out the most succulent grass, and the rasping sound of their tougues curling round large clumps before pulling them from the meadow.

When I eventually felt hot breath on the back of my neck I turned slowly and saw about twenty cows standing in a perfect arc. They had stopped grazing and were now gazing inquisitively at this peculiar creature sitting by the river on a pleasantly warm day, dressed in a waterproof coat, big boots and carrying a thin, tapered stick, a bag and a net. Their necks were stretched out and their heads lowered as they nudged each other slowly forward, their characteristic bovine curiosity taking over from their normal fear, although the ones furthest forward had straight, splayed legs dug well into the ground to avoid making too rapid progress. I felt rather like the conductor of an orchestra as they stood attentively watching me, although still somewhat apprehensively. I summoned my deepest and most authoritative voice.

'After three,' I commanded, lifting my arms as if to begin some great musical work. 'One . . . '

Before I could manage 'two', legs, feet and tails shot into the air and back at the same time. I could see the enquiring looks change to shock and horror at this unexpected outburst. After that I could not see what happened. Tears filled my eyes as I shook with helpless laughter at the rapid backward retreat and my ribs began to ache at the thought of the members of 'my orchestra' making such a quick and dramatic exit from my stage. When my eyes eventually cleared I saw that the objects of my amusement had regrouped and were in much the same formation as before, although by this time they were some distance away towards the middle of the field. The look of disgust and disdain on their faces was quite evident and I am sure it was not just a figment of my imagination. I began to laugh again when one cow, which I assumed to be the leader of the herd, looked at each of the others in turn. If I could have interpreted any communication between her and the others I am sure it would have been a rather scornful 'silly bugger'.

My gaze reverted to the river where the flies were floating down and I watched the way their course and speed were determined by the currents. Many were being funnelled into a long line as the water was channelled between weeds or boulders, and they gained speed in the faster-running narrowed flow. On the flat, calm reaches, submerged boulders, or tree branches blown into the river and carried down in some flood, impeded the steady flow, forming eddies and boils on the surface at regular intervals. I watched the glistening, dancing patterns they created and admired the effects of these involuntary underwater artists. In the flat, slow areas, the rings left by rising trout radiated gradually to the sides and downstream from their original position, but dispersed quickly in the faster bubbling channels.

I was watching one of these channels where the water was directed close to the bank by a gravel bed, presumably built up over many years, when it suddenly occurred to me that the flies swept along this particular path were disappearing. Where were they going? I awoke from my half-mesmerised state and, fully alert now, focused my attention on another fly which disappeared about halfway down the channel before it widened out and rejoined the main flow. The next fly disappeared in exactly the same spot, which I had marked by its relative positon to a tree on the bank. Occasionally a fly would travel past, but more often than not it looked as if they were swallowed up in some inexplicable way. I could

121

not see the tell-tale rings of the trout feeding and they were certainly not taking off, so where were they going?

I slid down the bank on bottom and elbows, hoping that the hobs in the heels of my boots would brake and control the rate of descent and stop me from sliding straight into the river. The idea behind this approach was to avoid being silhouetted against the skyline, but it meant that I had to keep re-adjusting my vest, shirt and coat which had an annoying tendency to ride up my back to at least shoulder-blade level.

Once down at water level, I made my way slowly and very carefully to the marked tree, which was the fourth one up in a line of about ten. It was remarkable how different the river seemed now, after viewing it from my elevated position on the bank, and it took me a few moments to find my bearings and the marked tree. The water looked deep in the channel; I tested it with my outstretched leg and came to the conclusion that there would be very little opportunity for wading. I bypassed the first tree in an awkward crouching posture that made my muscles ache, to avoid becoming entangled in the lower branches. Peering round this tree gave me a good view of the area I wanted to see. Sure enough, flies were disappearing at regular intervals, although still none of the movements associated with a feeding fish were evident. After some further discomfort I was round the next tree and much closer; I now had a clear view as I looked round the one remaining trunk. I could not believe my eyes when I saw a small part of a pointed snout break the surface and remove a fly without swirl or splash. I watched again. I could only just detect the faintest of dimples as yet another Mayfly was sipped from the surface. It was fascinating to watch the fish's mouth just breaking the surface from what must have been an almost vertical position in the water, gently and effortlessly satisfying its hunger.

Casting over the fish presented me with more problems. It was impossible to wade in the deep channel, which meant casting between the trees, although after my experiences

122

during the course of the morning I felt more confident. I found that by kneeling on the bank, sideways to the river, I could make just enough room for my arm to manipulate the rod. This was fine until the bag suddenly swung from my back and out over the river, which upset my balance quite considerably. The bag seemed determined that I should follow it, until I made a desperate, despairing grab with my free hand for the grass on the bank, which fortunately held and supported me so that an unwelcome head-first dive into the river was narrowly avoided. I had to concentrate very hard in order to regain my balance. I was suspended over the water with my bag swinging from my neck like a pendulum, and only a tuft of grass to hold on to, which I hoped and prayed would not give way. Carefully I pulled my shoulders back, so transferring the weight of the bag from the water to the bank, which restored my equilibrium.

I removed my bag before making further attempts to cast over the fish which was still sipping away merrily, oblivious of the disaster he had so nearly caused. As soon as I had cast my fly onto the river it automatically followed the channel down to the fish, where it disappeared in much the same manner as the natural ones, being taken neatly and delicately and with a minimum of fuss. Seconds later the reel was revolving at alarming speed. The ratchet screamed as the fish made a sudden and prolonged run for freedom, taking yards of line from the reel. Down the river he went before turning for some weeds. I applied pressure on the reel, which stopped him and made him turn and head back upstream. The speed with which he moved made it difficult for me to retrieve the loose line. I wondered if he would make a dive for the roots.

After what seemed an eternity, I began to take more and more control. He must be tiring now, I told myself, unclipping and flicking open the landing net. The fish's response was to make another dash downstream taking more line, although much more slowly and not so far this time. Eventually I had him some two yards in front of me, cruising round

123

on the surface and only occasionally jerking his head as he tried to shed the hook. Painstakingly and patiently I brought him closer and closer as I managed to retrieve more and more line. As I had found on previous occasions with other fish, he made one last, desperate bid to escape when he saw the net, before I finally landed him. I was trembling with excitement and felt weak at the knees when I realised that I had caught a majestic fish weighing some one and a half pounds, beautifully shaped, marked and coloured. It would be difficult to describe such a fish to George and Arnie so I reluctantly killed him and reverently placed him in my bag.

For me the thrill of deceiving the fish into taking the fly, feeling the first tug when I had made contact and the uncompromising battle which ensued, was far superior to the dream cherished by so many people of a fish sizzling in the pan and the delectable meal which follows. More often than not I returned my fish to the river, holding them in well-oxygenated streamy water while they recovered from the exhausting contest, and happily watched them swim gracefully and unhurriedly away, none the worse for their ordeal.

I wandered up to the car, to find George and Arnie relaxing on the bank.

'Why aren't you fishing?' I asked.

'Tired out from casting,' came the lethargic reply. They had managed to catch a couple of fish each, but they were both adamant that to cast another fly at that stage would be impossible. I had to admit to a certain amount of fatigue myself, although mine was not through constantly casting.

'Never mind, look at this,' I said, producing 'Sipper' from my bag.

'Beautiful,' commented Arnie.

'What a beauty!' echoed George, now sitting bolt upright.

'What a fish!' they gasped, all signs of their earlier tiredness gone.

'Yes, he's a splendid fish and he gave me a tremendous

124

fight,' I said, but I felt pangs of conscience as I looked at him lying motionless in the grass.

After a cup of tea and a little more substantial refreshment, we began fishing again, spurred on by the increased activity of the evening when more fish started to rise. I strolled off up the river, watching the now familiar but still riveting Mayfly dance and the obvious and ravenous thumping sound of a trout taking a Mayfly, emulating the descriptions in the books.

I watched the swallows pursuing their persistent and endless quest for food, and the water voles sitting on the banks, no doubt resting after a busy and hectic day. The sun was a huge fiery ball of orange making its way towards the horizon and the birds were singing in the trees, complementing the sound of the water rippling over the stones. Amid all this I could not help thinking from time to time of how many more fish were rising quietly and effectively in some hidden lie, although tiredness forced me to decide to search for these another day. I fished the evening in open water free from obstacles, much as I had always done, but my mind was awhirl with thoughts of what I had seen and how I had fished earlier that day. For the first time it felt as though I was hunting and stalking fish, following my inbred atavistic tendencies; it presented more of a challenge and required much more thought than the way I was fishing now, although even that was never easy. I was quite content standing in the river, in the calm and quiet of an early summer evening, listening to the water making music as it passed by my waders. I thanked the old man many times as I reflected on what an art fly fishing was and how much I had learned in one day, thanks to him.

CHAPTER THIRTEEN

Fishing was always interesting and absorbing, but for the two weeks after the Mayfly had finished it seemed something of an anticlimax. The river was noticeably quiet compared with the previous fortnight; the fish were far more restrained, rising less frequently, and they appeared to be fewer in number. Places where I had seen the water boiling with activity were now calm, disturbed only occasionally by an odd, lethargic-looking rise. Now and again I would find a fish persistently feeding, but most of them were presumably resting after the gluttonous orgy the large and abundant Mayfly had provided.

Fred had witnessed the spectacle many times before and was obviously prepared for this lack of activity. He was convinced that many of the fish we had seen rising had not fed on the surface since the previous year's Mayfly hatch and would not be seen again until the following year's hatch, quite content in the meantime to feed on worms washed from the banks, on minnows, and on other varieties of sub-surface food. It was interesting listening to Fred theorising, even rapturising about the events he recalled from his many years pursuing his hobby on the banks of the Derwent. The more I listened or discussed with him some aspect of fishing, the more I became aware that he never once, during his recollections of the past, implied that they were better days. He made comparisons, naturally. He remembered good years and bad and the particularly good or bad parts of certain years. He could recall a record catch during a certain June, or an April when he had not fished the fly at all because of persistent heavy water. He seemed content with what he had had then and more than content with what he had now. He looked forward rather than back and always found something positive to say, even when the Derwent was at its most frustrating. He used expressions such as, 'It'll be better in an hour or so when it warms up a little', or on a particularly bright day he would convince us that it would be fine once the sun dropped onto the hills later in the day. So it proved on some occasions, but sometimes, for some inexplicable reason, the fly hatch would remain sparse all day, with a corresponding lack of surface-feeding fish. I am sure Fred tried to reassure not only us but himself, too, with his natural and welcome optimism.

The first Saturday after June the sixteenth saw a dramatic change in our fishing on the Derwent. Syd arrived on its banks. The first indication we had that things might be different was Syd's tackle. We had decided to meet at George's which was the most central point when my car was being used, as it was on this Saturday. Invariably George and Arnie would be sitting on the wall at the front of George's house, eager and ready to be off. Next to them would be the rods neatly tied in their bags, two pairs of waders, two trout bags, two nets and other incidentals, all easily identifiable in a neat, regimented arrangement. As soon as the boot was opened, George efficiently and methodically transferred the equipment from the pavement to the boot. We could hear his slightly muffled voice from the back of the car as he checked everything in, including my tackle — 'Three rods, three pairs of waders, three nets, three bags, flasks, coats' and so on — until he was sure everything was securely packed. After this ritual was completed he would, without fail, turn to us and say, 'Have we forgotten anything?' followed by another look in the direction of the pavement where everything had been placed earlier. How many times they had been through every item before I arrived I could not imagine.

Syd arrived in a flurry of peeping horn, flashing headlights, squealing brakes and a hearty 'Morning, my beauties!' which was one of his favourite expressions for his friends but hardly applicable to us. He opened the boot with the same determination with which he had slammed the driver's door shut, and unceremoniously extricated his tackle from amongst the fire extinguishers, boxes and other paraphernalia connected with his work. George's face reflected disbelief and anxiety as Syd passed him an odd wader and a piece of a rod, followed by a bag and the other two sections of his rod. Another wader and a flask appeared, along with more bits and pieces, until Syd informed George that everything he required had been transferred to the boot of my car. He slammed his boot shut just as George was tentatively asking him if he was sure everything he needed was there. 'Sure, my old beauty, let's get moving.' Arnie was speechless, his expression radiating disgust and alarm at the irreverent way Syd treated such items of importance. My first rod did not have the luxury of a canvas bag, I thought, but at least it was kept together with pieces of string!

It was years since Syd had fished the Derwent. We listened to him describing parts of the river and some of the fish he had caught. We responded positively or negatively when he asked about certain aspects of the river or its immediate environment. He was obviously looking forward to his reunion with the river and a day in the fresh air, in the delightful surroundings he recalled so well. Nor had the prospect of joining us for a pint or two at the end of the day escaped his thoughts; all these things, he told us, were the necessary ingredients for the perfect day.

Our journey to the river along the by now familiar roads seemed to take less time than usual, with the added novelty of Syd's conversation. We were soon at the car park surveying the scene.

'What a beautiful morning!' bellowed Syd, beating his chest in Tarzan fashion, which rather startled us. We always approached the river in a far more circumspect and reverent manner and, no matter how excited we were by the sight of rising fish, our voices never rose above a loud whisper.

Syd gave the river a quick, casual look and followed this with several exaggerated gulps of fresh air before diving towards the boot which I had opened so that George could remove the tackle. He was horrified at Syd's imminent involvement. Arnie and I had come to accept, quite willingly, that George had the responsibility of loading and unloading the boot, and we would never have dared to interfere. We stood back smiling as George placed a bag on the ground and whipped round, barring Syd's way.

'Just a minute! I know where everything is, so leave it to me,' he said, as diplomatically as he could. Having seen the way Syd had taken the tackle from his own boot, I could understand his alarm.

Eventually we were all tackled up and ready. We agreed on the time we would meet for lunch, and Syd informed us that he was heading for the top end of the river where he remembered a brook running into the Derwent.

'Be careful there. The fish have a reputation for jumping back into the river,' I said, with a glance at Arnie to remind him of his slippery fish.

'Will you be all right?' asked George with a note of apprehension in his voice.

'Fine, me beauty,' came the reply, and Syd departed, making his way upstream in a very purposeful way.

George soon followed him, leaving Arnie and me by the car until Arnie decided he was going to have a walk downstream. I knew George would be up on what we called 'the shallows', some two hundred yards upstream. I might as well have an amble up in that direction, I thought to myself, with a distinct feeling of pleasure at having that sort of freedom. Whether to wander upstream or downstream; to fish seriously or merely to watch; to sit, semi-recumbent, on the bank, watching the cows grazing and the birds wheeling overhead or flying at low level over the river — it was all for me to choose. One of my favourite occupations, which had become something of an obsession, was to pick up the song of a bird and try to locate the singer's position. Sometimes it was a while before I could find the speck of a skylark high in a clear sky, or a bluetit flitting about in a particular tree. I used to feel satisfied and contented when I made a quick observation and would then make my way confidently into the river to take on a fish with what must have been a supercilious grin on my face. A certain lack of concentration on the fishing would prevail, however, when the location of my quarry had eluded me. The birds seemed to enjoy the game, much to my annoyance. Sometimes, I am sure, they played hide and seek, disappearing behind a branch and remaining quiet until I thought they had flown to another tree. As soon as I had given up or averted my gaze, a quick 'Chirp, chirp' from the tree would have me peering up once more. Silence again before I could hear 'Chirp, chirp' a few feet higher in the tree, and again I would be straining to see where the call had come from. If I could not find the hiding place, my feeling of frustration sometimes nearly made me resort to tossing a stone gently into the tree to force an exit, but I always resisted the temptation and tried to accept my defeat graciously.

Slowly I progressed up the river until I found George who was casting over numerous fish both to his left and right as he stood more or less in the centre of the river. It was interesting to watch the way he handled the rod. I was very impressed when he completely changed direction from one side of the river to the other, my eye following the arc of the fly line before it drove the leader forward, gently settling the fly lightly onto the river. He would only occasionally catch the water on the back-cast, which destroyed his timing and made the line concertina and land heavily.

A figure walking down the river some distance away caught my eye. It was not Fred's gait which I had come to recognise quite easily by now. A stranger, perhaps. After a while I recognised the figure as Syd. He's back in good time, I thought, unless he is going downstream for an hour. When he drew level George asked how he was getting on.

'Lost me flies, my beauty,' was the reply.

'Lost what?' asked George.

'My flies!' shouted Syd.

George retrieved his line and began making his way to the bank. Conversation from river to bank while standing in rough, fast water was difficult if not impossible. The noise of water rushing through and round one's waders and from the wake they created, reduced one's ability to pick up any sounds except those in the immediate vicinity.

I joined Syd on the bank at about the same time as George. It was not long before he was graphically describing his morning's fishing and the way he had lost his two flies high up in a tree. We enquired why he had not tied on new ones. Abjectly he admitted that he had left his glasses in the car and could not manage without them. Then he confessed that because of his failing eyesight he always tied his flies on at home and attached the leader to the fly line when he arrived on the river. Being totally preoccupied with our own preparations, we had not noticed this.

Syd readily accepted my offer of help. He hunted through the assortment of boxes lying at the bottom of his bag until he found a green tobacco tin from which the maker's name had long since been obliterated with constant friction and handling. From this he produced two flies and gratefully asked me if I would tie them onto the leader for him.

The feathers from which the flies were made were very soft compared with ours. Syd confirmed that they were wet fly patterns and told us that he always 'fished wet'. This method was completely different from our approach. Whereas we fished upstream with the fly floating towards us on the surface, a wet fly is cast and fished downstream. The flies we used were tied with the stiff feathers from the cape

HACKLE: BLACK HEN   WING: PART OF GROUSE WING

TAIL: GOLDEN PHEASANT TIPPETS

BODY: SEAL'S FUR DYED CLARET
RIBBED WITH GOLD WIRE

GROUSE AND CLARET WINGED WET FLY

of a cock bird, which we treated with silicone from time to time to assist buoyancy, while the wet flies are tied with the softer, more downy feathers from a hen bird and left untreated, to allow them to absorb water and sink. We only fished one fly at any one time, whereas the wet fly fisherman uses two or three patterns tied onto the leader at intervals. This gives variation in the depth at which the flies are presented and a choice of size and colour. The flies are cast across and down the river at about thirty degrees to the fisherman; they then sink and travel back in an arc from the bank, coming to rest at a point in line with and below the fisherman. The idea then is to take a pace downstream and cast again at the same angle, progressing slowly and methodically so that the whole river is covered by the flies in a succession of swinging arcs. It is assumed that many fish are feeding underneath the surface unobserved, which will take a submerged fly just as a surface-feeding fish will take a floating one.

It proved impossible to tie the flies onto the leader. What breaking strain nylon Syd was using I did not know, but it was far too thick to go through the eye of the fly. Even if it had gone through, a knot with that large diameter nylon would have looked like a piece of rope when tied to a relatively small fly. Syd did not have a spare leader, so I replaced his with one of mine which had a three-pound breaking strain. This time the nylon went effortlessly through the eye of the end fly — or tail fly, as it is known — and just as easily when I tied the second fly to the dropper which was probably some six-pound breaking strain nylon. The dropper is a short piece of nylon which extends from the leader at a joint where the strength of the nylon is increased to give it a taper. A leader may have several sections of nylon from the end where the last fly is attached, increasing in strength to the loop which joins it to the fly line and where the breaking strain of the nylon may be some twelve pounds or so. If this taper did not occur, the difference between the light nylon and the heavy fly line would result in the line snapping at this joint under the slightest pressure from fish, bank or tree.

When I had made sure everything was back in order I suggested to Syd that a visit to the tackle shop might be prudent, to purchase some leaders. He thanked me profusely and we chatted for a while before it was time to head back to the car for lunch.

About halfway through the afternoon, Fred arrived at the part of the river where I was sitting enjoying a refreshing drink of tea. We exchanged ideas on what fly the fish were taking and where we had seen most fish rising. Further upstream he had seen George and Arnie who, he said, were struggling to arouse any interest from the fish. He then went on to tell me that he had seen a stranger on the river.

'What did he look like?' I asked.

'I couldn't really tell,' replied Fred, 'he was curled up on the bank with his head resting on a fishing bag and his face covered with a hat. I'll tell you one thing, if he rolls over once he'll be in the river.'

'Sounds like Syd,' I said, and told Fred about the new member and that he had come with us.

I made my way up river casting over various fish.

Occasionally one would swirl casually underneath the fly, but it was one of those days when nothing seemed to tempt the fish. I tried almost every pattern in the box, grey ones, blue ones, green ones and black ones, all to no avail. It was fishing at its most frustrating, but the peace and quiet and the beauty of the surroundings more than compensated for the lack of interest displayed by the fish. Eventually I came across George and Arnie, who were enjoying a smoke and reflecting on the inconsiderate nature of fish.

'How have you fared?' asked George.

I told them ruefully that every fish that had risen had done so with a premeditated and determined effort to goad me into the water and then deliberately annoy me by refusing repeatedly to take my fly. 'I saw at least two fish laughing at my fly patterns as they floated overhead,' I went on, 'and I saw at least one fish wink knowingly at another close by after looking in my direction.'

'It almost seems like that sometimes,' agreed Arnie.

George and Arnie had remained close to the car after the break for lunch. They had not seen Syd, but had heard from Fred of the sleeping stranger on the bank.

'I'll go and see what he's up to,' I said, leaving them contentedly sending smoke signals to some unidentified tribe on the other side of the valley. Laughing, winking, thinking fish! Tribes of Indians in rural Derbyshire! This fresh air and solitude must be extremely intoxicating stuff, I contemplated, stumbling along the uneven bank in my search for Syd.

It was quite some time before I spotted his familiar stocky frame fishing in a fast, bubbling, swirling stretch of water with his team of submerged flies. His progress down the river was slow. As well as casting and waiting for the flies to finish tracing an arc from the bank, each step forward had to be taken with care. The river bottom must have been very uneven, judging by the way Syd made cautious side-steps every so often to avoid what must have been hidden boulders. I could see that the depth varied tremendously, too: in some places the water level was only at knee height, then after a couple of paces it was barely an inch below the top of his waders. I could see how dramatically the water pressure increased at this depth by the much longer wake extending downstream from his almost invisible wader-clad legs.

Eventually he reached a point where the depth prevented any further progression downstream. The water was equally deep between him and the bank, which left him with no option but to retrace his steps to the point where he had gained access to the river. His progress as he pressed against the current looked fraught with danger, for often the pressure of the water forced what appeared to be involuntary movements when he lifted one of his feet. Whenever this happened he would hastily replace it on the bed of the river to restore his balance before trying a different route. I could judge the security of the position by his facial expressions and the way he used his arms. A confident smile after passing one obstacle was often followed by an expression of horror when a deep hole or large boulder had to be circumnavigated. At this point Syd resembled one of those people whose duty it is to guide a plane down onto the deck of an aircraft carrier by gesticulating with fluorescent discs. Having been in that situation many times myself, I knew how Syd must be feeling. I was as relieved as he was when he reached the safety of the bank, and just as tired. From my safe vantage point I had been struggling with him every step of the way.

'Phew! that was a little close at times,' exclaimed Syd when he eventually saw me and joined me on the bank. 'Mind you, it wouldn't have been the first time I'd had a ducking.' He went on to tell me about fishing a river in the south while he was on business in the area. The river had been quite overgrown and he had asked if he could remove some of the offending branches. He was given approval for this and began clearing a particular stretch until there was only one overhanging branch left. To reach it he had to climb the tree and stand on the branch before he could begin sawing. He did not realise that he was standing on the part of the branch which he was removing from the main trunk. The next thing he knew, he had descended into the river at a fair rate of knots. When he scrambled to his feet he noticed the river immediately around him was tinged with red. He described his visit to the hospital where he received several stitches in his thumb and thigh which had been gashed by the slate which formed much of the river bed and the bankside.

'The funny thing was,' went on Syd, his eyes filling with water and his shoulders beginning to shake, 'that when I arrived back at the hotel, having abandoned any immediate desire to fish, I slammed the car door shut on my good thumb, which meant another visit to the hospital and more stitches.' The picture he painted of himself, limping out of the hospital with both thumbs heavily bandaged, made me helpless with laughter. Syd pointed to the scars on his thumbs to corroborate his story, but whether they had been inflicted then or on some other, more mundane and less humorous occasion, only Syd will ever know.

When our laughter had subsided I asked Syd if he was tired from the afternoon's exercise. I am sure he was about to reply in the affirmative, when he must have noticed a knowing expression on my face. He then admitted that after lunch the warm sun, together with the noise of the dappling water, had weighed heavily on his eyelids and he had succumbed to the temptation of a brief sleep.

'Mind you,' he said, 'I had the fright of my life when I woke up. I turned over before I realised quite where I was and finished up about a foot from the edge of the river!'

'You weren't much further away while you were asleep, according to Fred,' I said. 'In fact he says that you were so close and so deeply asleep that your snoring was making waves on the water and stopping fish rising for yards either side.'

'You're joking!' exclaimed Syd.

'I might be, Syd,' I said, 'I might be.'

We ambled back down the river, content and at peace with the world. I could see smoke idly reaching for the sky from some of the cottages dotted on the hillsides, presumably lit to compensate for the cooler air of a late summer evening.

George and Arnie were already at the car and beginning to replace flies in boxes and reels in bags.

'Just put everything of yours next to mine, Syd, I'll see to the rest,' offered George.

'He'll have him well trained in a fortnight,' I remarked to Arnie as I thankfully relieved my legs of a pair of necessary yet awkward pieces of regalia.

The evening at the Chequers naturally revolved around Syd. We asked him whether he had found the day enjoyable and how it compared with his old memories of it. Some of the regulars enquired, although it was quite obvious, whether Syd had been with us. Bert, the landlord, chipped in as usual from time to time, suggesting that he would suffer if he joined our company.

'You'll never be the same again,' he jibed.

'I'll risk it whatever the consequences,' retorted Syd. 'It'll be well worth it after the day I've had.' This rendered Bert speechless for a time, which was very gratifying.

The conversation went casually and reflectively on until I went to the bar. George, Arnie and I drank bitter, while Syd preferred mild, so in order to create as little confusion as possible I passed our three tankards over to Bert separately.

'Three bitters in these, please, and a mild for "Rip Van Winkle" in that one,' delaying passing Syd's over until he had begun to fill ours.

'Rip Van who?' exploded Bert.

'Winkle,' I said, 'which reminds me, I'll have to go round the back' (this was the expression we used for the toilet, which happened to be outside and across the car park).

When I returned, Syd was in full cry, describing to everyone who would listen how he had nearly drowned after falling asleep on the bank.

'Shouldn't be sleeping while you're fishing, should you?' Bert asked a perfect stranger whom he was supposed to be serving at the time. The man looked quite startled and did not seem to know how or whether to answer.

'Rumour has it that he has blown every moorhen off the surface of the river for yards and frightened every trout, which were last seen heading down the river for Matlock,' I said, hoping to relieve the stranger of any embarrassment at being brought into our conversation.

'No wonder,' chimed in Bert, determined to be part of the scene instead of looking after his customers.

'Hell fire!' spluttered Arnie suddenly as he took the top off his beer. 'That's mild!'

'And you have my tankard,' said George, looking at me.

We shuffled the drinks round, at the same time complimenting Bert on his efficiency. Deep down we knew Bert was a good landlord who always kept a very good cellar. I suppose the length of time we had known him enabled the banter to flow freely between us, although on many occasions he did set himself up as a target for derision. He always seemed to take it in good part, however, and was never offended by our cryptic comments. As always, after one or two more pints, when we had retold and relived some of our experiences, we forgave him for his indiscretion.

CHAPTER FOURTEEN

Syd fished with us every Saturday, and gradually we began to realise that he was not quite as knowledgeable as we had first thought and not as serious about fishing as we were. He could cast effectively, from what we observed on the occasions when we happened to see him, and he had impressed us when he demonstrated the technique during our initiation session on Arnie's lawn. He was not, however, very familiar with fly patterns and not over-conscientious about the way he treated his tackle and looked after his equipment; nevertheless, he thoroughly enjoyed just being there. Whether he was fishing or whether we were, he always wanted to stop for a chat — which was also a good excuse for a pipe of tobacco. Fortunately Fred immediately took to Syd, and they could often be seen some distance away, silhouetted against the skyline, nodding and gesticulating as they talked. Fred was not a particularly demonstrative sort of fellow, but some of Syd's antics made him chuckle freely.

The afternoon siesta was a ritual that we came to accept, after the first Saturday when we had thought it quite unusual. Depending on the weather, Syd would choose an open bank, a sheltered hollow or the shade from a convenient tree, emerging like some gopher once the urge to sleep had been satisfied. I suppose during the day he spent proportionately more time chatting, sleeping, eating, drinking and smoking than he did fishing, which to him was only an incidental part of the day as a whole.

On one particular Saturday he did not fish at all. Despite all George's efforts to train him to be slightly more methodical and punctilious, he always seemed to forget or misplace something — glasses on the very first Saturday; teabags on another Saturday. If he remembered the teabags and the flask of hot water, he was liable to leave his beaker behind, making it impossible for him to have a drink unless he was close to one of us, when he could always share ours.

We were chatting away merrily as we usually did before a day's fishing, full of confidence and eager to resume our association with the river after what seemed like an eternity, although it was only seven days. Syd was at the wheel on this occasion, turning round from time to time to address Arnie and me in the back, which considerably alarmed Arnie who was not the best of passengers. Some dark, ominous-looking clouds were gathering on the hills through which the river ran, and we had decided that we were in for a wetting.. It was then I realised that Syd was not wearing his hat, which was a tweed variety, with a peak at the front and back. A fishing hat to Syd was like a helmet to a policeman. It was part of his dress, matching his coat, well-pressed corduroy trousers and highly polished shoes. Even if he did not fish very seriously or successfully, he looked the part, and his photograph would certainly have graced the pages of *Derbyshire Life*, along with any other member of the county's gentry.

'Where's your hat?' I asked him. Syd felt the top of his head, and then did so again and again, displaying an exaggerated self-consciousness when he realised he was not wearing it. 'Must be in the boot, me beauty,' he said, looking in the driving mirror for visual confirmation of what I and his hand had told him. As soon as we arrived at the car park George looked in the boot, but failed to find the missing hat.

'Where's my spare rod top?' Syd asked him, for George was by now fully in charge of all the gear, even when we were using Syd's car for transport.

'I'm sure I've taken everything out,' said George, returning to the boot just to make sure.

'Why did you want the spare?' asked Arnie.

Syd pointed to a ferrule which was loose in the whippings, making the whole rod impossible to use. Usually, by pooling our resources we could help Syd out — tying on his flies, lending him some teabags or a cup or even a spare pair of fishing socks — but a spare rod defeated us completely.

'What are you going to do?' asked George who was always, by his very nature, concerned when anything was not quite as it should be.

'I could go and fetch it,' mused Syd, 'but I won't bother,' he decided, after wandering around and looking amongst the bags, coats, nets and shoes which were still lined up in an orderly manner by the car.

'It isn't there,' said Arnie, picking up his bag, placing it on his shoulder and adjusting the strap to ensure maximum comfort.

'I know,' said Syd, 'I'm looking for my belt.'

'Don't tell me you've left that as well!' cried George, trying hard to suppress his annoyance and exasperation. I could understand this, knowing George as well as I did. He would be worried and ill at ease all day, thinking that one of us was deprived of a day's fishing — which was, after all, the reason for our presence there.

'I should imagine there's more of your equipment at home than there is here, if the truth were known,' I suggested.

'Must have been good ale last night,' muttered Syd, giving a last desperate glance into the boot and holding up his waders with his hands which were acting as substitutes for the missing belt.

Arnie suggested that Syd should stay with him and use his rod from time to time.

'No thanks, me old beauty; besides, I must dash, see you later.' Seconds later he had negotiated the stile leading into the field above the car park and was running up the fence side of the field which was opposite and well away from the river. Running in waders is difficult at the best of times, even

141

without the disadvantage of nowhere to anchor the straps that hold them up.

'Where's he off to?' asked George, his face beginning to show the slightest indication of a smile. Syd was rolling and swaying, his sense of balance obviously impaired by the lack of movement in his arms, which were locked gorilla fashion in a desperate attempt to keep his waders in place. Several young beasts in the field looked horrified, while others seemed bewildered at the sudden apparition. Usually they did nothing more than give us a casual glance, but more often than not they chose to ignore us completely.

'It must have been good beer last night,' I commented, when it became apparent that Syd was heading for a barn in the corner of the field. He disappeared through the open door, releasing his waders with a distinct display of urgency. Seconds later, out of the door careered two more beasts, their tails vertical and their legs kicking. By this time we three were helpless, clutching the fence for support. 'Shades of Boroughbridge,' choked Arnie. He was still muttering something about feeling weak at the knees when we finally thought about moving off to do some fishing.

The sport during the morning was very good, with plenty of fish rising. I immediately caught a fish on a Blue Dun, which was most unusual although very gratifying. Must have made a good selection of fly, I thought, moving slowly and carefully towards the next fish which was rising beautifully in a stickle in the water created by the partially submerged roots of a tree at the edge of the bank. There he was, sipping flies eagerly and persistently, completely unaware of my presence. I watched him for a while before flicking a fly over his nose. My arm was poised and raised ready to strike. I stared in disbelief when the fly passed over him and down towards me on the current. He was still rising freely, which prompted me to think he could not have seen my fly. My next cast sent the fly about two feet above him, which should give him a little more time to see it. Down it floated round the tree, following the current until it was over the feeding trout. Nothing. The fly continued harmlessly down on the current. Still the fish was rising. I decided to give him one more try, although there was no reason why he should take it this time. The confidence of a few moments before was beginning to evaporate. Sure enough, he showed not the slightest interest.

I reeled in the line and changed my Blue Dun for a Ginger Quill. As well as a complete contrast in colours, as the names suggest, there was a marked difference in the shape of the body. The Blue Dun body was tied with part of a heron's wing with yellow silk segmenting it, whereas the Ginger Quill body was tied with a single strand of a peacock eye feather with all the hair removed. Consequently the body of the Blue Dun was grey, fat and quite fluffy and spiralled with yellow, while that of the Ginger Quill was flat and smooth and barred black and white.

I applied a dab of fly oil to prevent the feathers getting water-logged, and then the fly was airborne, settling on the water just in front of the fish. A sudden swirl, a quick strike and I had hooked the fish which took off up the river before turning and leaping out of the water. I felt the line go slack when the fish splashed down, shedding the hook as it did so. I was left with a sinking feeling in the pit of my stomach, until I philosophically wished him the best of luck and made a mental note of where he had been rising, for future reference.

Two fish hooked and two fly patterns used was the best record since the end of the Mayfly hatch. This sort of pattern developed throughout the morning, although not alternating like the first two fish. The next two swirled at the Ginger Quill, showing interest, but refused to rise again, presumably having frightened themselves at being so very nearly deceived by my artificial fly. The next fish ignored it completely but rose to the Blue Dun as soon as I had replaced and presented it. Quite amazing, I thought, trying to determine why certain fish preferred a certain fly. There must have been at least

143

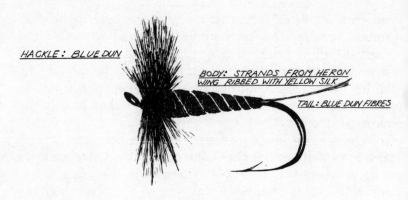

HACKLE: BLUE DUN

BODY: STRANDS FROM HERON WING RIBBED WITH YELLOW SILK

TAIL: BLUE DUN FIBRES

BLUE DUN

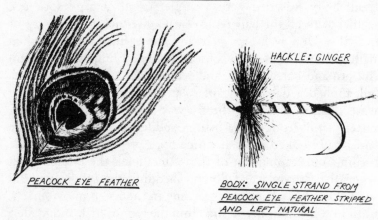

PEACOCK EYE FEATHER

HACKLE: GINGER

BODY: SINGLE STRAND FROM PEACOCK EYE FEATHER STRIPPED AND LEFT NATURAL

GINGER QUILL

two distinct flies hatching, although I could not detect the difference between them. If that was the case, why should one fish prefer one species while another fish, which was only yards away, preferred to feed on a different one? It was not as though a particular fly was peculiar to one part of the river. Whether they took the Blue Dun or the Ginger Quill was quite haphazard.

How fickle fish were, I mused as I sat on the bank, having a welcome cup of coffee and what I thought was a well-earned

144

rest. No two days were alike. One day, despite numerous fish feeding, I could spend hours casting over them with every fly in the box and not one would show the slightest interest. Another day, like today, the very first cast I made would produce a fish or at least signs of interest. This always gave me a false sense of well-being and led me to believe that I would catch every subsequent fish, assuming in my own mind that I had made the correct choice of fly which would hold me in good stead for the day. Sometimes, after the first burst of activity, hours would pass before another fish would show the slightest movement towards the fly. Today the trout were showing continued interest in two patterns, which meant good sport.

I tried to put myself in the fishes' position, lying in the river feeling very hungry and with a choice of food floating down towards me at regular intervals. What would I do, supposing the food was beef and lamb? Would I select my favourite meat to feed on, ignoring the other completely and hoping that the supply would continue, or would I feed on both, or choose my favourite but occasionally try the second offering? I came to the conclusion that if I were really hungry I would feed on both varieties until my hunger was beginning to be satisfied, when I would feed only on my preferred choice. I also decided that the fish did not think as I did, which was probably a good thing. If they did and fed on anything and everything all the time, fishing would be easy, lacking in skill, effort, thought and knowledge; there would be no need to gain any experience to achieve success and the satisfaction and pride which comes with it. A very different satisfaction and pride, I contemplated, when I recalled my cricketing days. My failure to score as a batsman would leave me feeling guilty. On the other hand, brilliantly dismissing one of the opposition or scoring a half-century and receiving the congratulations of team mates and spectators alike, enhanced the achievement and I enjoyed the temporary glory.

Fishing is about many of these things, but the fundamental

difference is that it is so personal and does not require other people for it to be enjoyed. My achievement or lack of it concerned only me; it was a duel with the river and the elements. Personal pride was involved because only I knew what had been achieved when I ultimately netted a fish — unless by chance someone with at least some knowledge of fly fishing happened to be watching. Discomfort, effort, skill and the recall of experience were all required to produce total satisfaction. Conversely, a feeling of defeat came when the reward for such endeavour resulted in failure, although this feeling was only temporary. If it were not for these emotions I would probably be following some other sport or pastime today. As it is, the sport is a blend of many feelings: admiration for the environment; the beauty of an everchanging landscape; the smell of grass after a shower of rain or the scent from wild flowers fanned by a gentle breeze; a high regard for my quarry; a feeling of pride and achievement after a day of battering wind and rain; a feeling of annoyance at losing a fish close to the net, or elation at deceiving and landing a fish from a difficult position. The thought of joining the others afterwards, to mull over the events, made the day and the sport complete.

It's a pity that everyone can't share what I have, went through my mind as I sat watching the scene and feeling very privileged to be part of it; but then I realised that other people must enjoy their pastimes just as much as I did mine. If not, the river banks would be over-crowded and no one would be playing — depending upon the season — cricket, football or hockey, or would be walking, horse-riding, painting or any of the other hundred and one things people do for a hobby. I must have spent a great deal of time thinking, for when I looked at my watch it showed the time we had arranged to meet for lunch.

Althouth it only took me ten minutes or so to reach the car, George and Arnie were already there, patiently waiting.

'Sorry I'm late,' I said. 'And how have you got on this morning?'

'Unbelievable,' said Arnie. 'Plenty of fish rising and taking my fly, which makes a pleasant change. I've caught three and lost several.'

'Superb,' echoed George. 'Although I've only landed one fish the sport has been tremendous.'

'What fly were you using?' I asked. They had both been using a Kite's Imperial throughout the morning and had not suffered the inconvenience at having to change flies at regular intervals as I had. 'I must try that this afternoon,' I said, after describing my experiences of the morning.

'Where's Syd?' asked George, which made us all suddenly aware of his absence. 'I haven't seen him at all this morning, have you?' He sounded a little concerned. The last we had seen of him had been his hurrying figure disappearing into the farm building.

'I hope he's all right,' said Arnie after we had finished lunch, which was probably half an hour later.

'He can't have fallen in,' said George, 'because he isn't fishing.'

'He could have fallen in while he was asleep,' I suggested. 'Mind you, it's funny we haven't seen anything of him at all.'

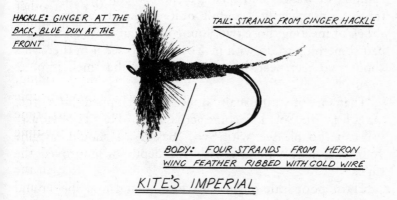

HACKLE: GINGER AT THE BACK, BLUE DUN AT THE FRONT

TAIL: STRANDS FROM GINGER HACKLE

BODY: FOUR STRANDS FROM HERON WING FEATHER RIBBED WITH GOLD WIRE

KITE'S IMPERIAL

We were becoming quite worried, almost to the point of going in search of him, when we spotted a diminutive figure in the distance, some two fields away.

'Can't be sure, but I think that's him,' I said. 'At least, it's someone in waders and without a rod or anything.'

'Yes, it is him,' said Arnie when he was much closer. Syd came diagonally across the field towards us, whistling merrily and with a jaunty step, obviously unaware that he had caused us any concern at all.

'Hello, me old beauties, I see you've had lunch,' he said cheerily.

'I should think we have, since we arranged to meet an hour ago,' said George, in a manner which expressed both annoyance that he was late and relief that he was all right.

'What have you been doing?' asked Arnie.

'Well . . . ' said Syd, unwrapping his sandwiches and preparing a drink.

'At least you've managed to bring that with you today,' I said, grabbing the opportunity to comment in the hope that it would persuade him to be less scatterbrained. Syd gave me a sideways look and chuckled before continuing.

'It was like this,' he went on. 'As you know, the call of nature came over me very urgently, so I decided to make for the barn in the corner of the field. It was very difficult running in waders and trying to hold them up at the same time. Consequently I didn't quite make it, although the shock of meeting those two young beasts in there might have had something to do with it. You want to see it in there, it's about two feet deep in cow muck and the smell is quite awful.'

'That sort of stuff usually does smell,' chipped in George, 'or at least, the sort I've come across does.' He was obviously still not too pleased with Syd. 'Besides, I should imagine your visit hasn't helped with the depth or improved the smell.'

'Those poor little buggers have to go and find shelter and

sleep in there,' I said, pointing to a group of innocent-looking cattle.

'It makes you feel sorry for them,' said Arnie. 'Fancy walking round a field all day with nothing to do but eat grass, and then having to walk into that lot. They have my sympathy.'

By this time Syd was finding it impossible to eat or drink. Every time he tried to take a bite from one of his sandwiches he almost choked with laughter. When he did manage to pick up his cup he shook most of the contents out of it. It was not very fair of us to remind him, when he had more or less composed himself, of the pheasants at Boroughbridge.

'How do you account for the rest of the time?' asked Arnie when the frivolity had subsided.

'You didn't spend the morning in the shed admiring your handiwork, did you?' asked George cynically, still smarting from the worry Syd had caused him. This is building up into one of Syd's stories, I thought, amid the bursts of laughter. The whole of the Chequers is going to hear about this whether they like it or not, and probably more than once.

'I was in a bit of a predicament,' Syd said, determined to carry on with his story. 'I had to take off my underpants, but before that I had to remove my waders, socks and trousers, which was extremely difficult, as you can imagine, in a shed full of cow muck and only lit by a single door.'

'How did you manage?' I asked, 'without getting your socks in the same state as your underwear?'

'Well, I had a walk round and found the most solid-looking spot,' Syd went on. 'Then I took off one wader and laid it out flat, which gave me a platform to stand on. Mind you, it was touch and go sometimes, pirouetting on one leg, but I managed pretty well until I replaced my waders, which were more of a khaki colour than green. It was difficult pulling them on with my hands slipping on wet . . . '

'All right,' said George, 'I've only just had something to eat.'

'If anyone had looked in they would have had a shock,' said Syd. 'It wasn't much better when I walked to the river. Just imagine meeting someone with waders and hands covered in cow muck, carrying a pair of dirty Y-fronts.'

Arnie and I were almost helpless by this time and even George could not restrain himself. 'What did you do?' he asked.

Syd told us how he had waded into the river as far as he could go and washed his hands, waders and Y-fronts.

'Oh no!' I gasped.

'What's the matter?' asked Arnie.

'You two have been upstream of Syd while I have been downstream. Just think what has floated past me this moring,' feigning disgust at the very thought. 'A bit of cow muck I can tolerate, but the thought of what came off those Y-fronts is more than even I can stand.'

Determined not to be sidetracked, Arnie asked, 'What happened to the rest of the time? It must have been mid-morning by the time you were cleaned up and yet you arrived here at two, an hour late for lunch.'

'Well,' said Syd, 'I couldn't walk about with a pair of wet pants in my hand, so I hung them in a tree to dry, which meant sitting waiting nearby. I must have nodded off to sleep for quite a while because they were nice and dry when I woke up. I knew you had gone upstream so I came to look for you, but before I found you I came across Fred on his way to the Square and Compass for his midday pint. He persuaded me to go with him.'

'Persuaded?' queried George.

'Well, asked me if I would like to join him.'

This was more than George could stand. 'You mean to tell me that while we have been concerned about you being unable to fish and worried when you were late for lunch, you were sitting in the pub sneaking a pint!' he bellowed.

'I'm afraid so, me old beauty,' chuckled Syd.

Poor George! I am sure it was the fact that Syd had stolen

a pint which really upset him. Arnie and I were not too pleased, either, although we did not take the matter quite so much to heart.

'I suppose you're going to sleep it off now,' I suggested sarcastically.

'I might just do that,' retorted Syd. 'Anyway, it's about time you began fishing again, isn't it?'

'I think we'd better,' I said, judging that it might have a calming effect on George's blood pressure.

Arnie decided to head downstream to where I had been fishing in the morning. George and I kept together more or less: he left me to have a go at the first fish and then entered the water some distance above me, but clearly visible. I had meant to change my fly to the Kite's Imperial, but the lunchtime activity had destroyed my capacity for any serious thought. Out of the corner of my eye I could see George casting vigorously over a fish, while I was trying to tempt a freely rising trout. I was not too concerned when my fish did not accept the fly because the morning had told me that a change of pattern would bring just reward. It suddenly occurred to me that George was not having the same kind of sport he had experienced that morning, although this might be only a temporary lapse. Then I saw him fumbling in his bag and taking out a fly box. It looked as though the Imperial had gone back into the box. I watched him snipping the nylon and then tying on another fly before casting again. This prompted me to change my Ginger Quill back to the Blue Dun to see what happened. The result was the same as before: the fly floated harmlessly over the fish and down the river before I retrieved the line, lifted the rod and cast again. The fly floated down again with no evidence of drag, so I could only assume that the morning's diet had changed completely, and this was more or less confirmed when I saw George making yet another change of fly.

Fred appeared from upstream where he, too, had had reasonable sport in the morning but had found things difficult after lunch, although I did suggest to him that fraternising with Syd might have had something to do with his failure.

'How does he do it? asked Fred.

'I honestly don't know,' I replied, 'but I sometimes wonder if he doesn't do it just for effect. Nobody could be so absent-minded — although having said that, I haven't met anyone quite like Syd before.'

'Neither have I,' echoed George who had joined us, having temporarily given up the struggle.

George and I could not believe the sudden change from the sport we had enjoyed during the morning to the total lack of it during the afternoon. The Derwent had been like that as long as Fred had known it; he suggested that if you could catch trout on the Derwent you could catch them anywhere and that they were the most educated fish he had come across. He left us with that thought, which George and I certainly could not dispute.

We decided to finish a little earlier than usual because of Syd's inactivity, and it was not until we were about to return to the car that I hooked another fish. I cast fly after fly over the rising trout. I stopped fishing from time to time, peering in an attempt to see what fly they were feeding on. It just so happened that during one of these observation sessions, the sun's rays percolating through the branches of a tree nicely highlighted where a trout was feeding. It was almost as though he was on stage, illuminated by a single spotlight against a dark background. Natural flies floated over him which he left alone, only rising at what appeared to me to be nothing. Then I noticed tiny dark specks drifting down towards him. Sure enough, every time one went over him it disappeared in a swirl. I looked at the surface of the river close to me and saw the same black flies, very small compared with the normal olives which hatched in great numbers. I fumbled through my fly box and found a size sixteen Black Gnat, which was the smallest fly in my collection. Even when it had been tied in place and dropped onto the water immediately in front of me, its size compared with those small black flies was quite astonishing. In the box my fly looked small, but on the river it took on gigantic proportions beside the other tiny black specks. It was almost time to leave, so I thought there would be nothing to lose with one last cast. I was amazed. The trout viciously took the offering as if it had been waiting for that particular fly all day.

George must have been watching, although I had not seen him on the bankside and was quite unaware of his presence.

'What did he take?' he enquired inquisitively, suggesting to me that he had not found the right pattern.

'A small Black Gnat,' I replied, at the same time trying to put some pressure on the fish to prevent him from diving into a weed bed. The pressure I exerted was not sufficient. The fish was soon in amongst the weed, tangling my line amongst the waving strands. I saw his silver underbelly flash once when he rolled tantalisingly near the surface. That was the last I saw of him. The line went taut and lifeless, which, from past experience, meant that the fly had been left in the weeds.

'Hard luck,' George commiserated.

'Never mind, at least I have managed to hook another fish. That's the first one since this morning.'

'That's one more than I've had,' said George, which confirmed my earlier suspicions. Two figures ambled up towards us looking leg-weary but quite contented. Arnie was tired with casting and changing fly patterns, which suggested that the lower reaches were no different from where George and I had been fishing. Syd was tired out with watching Arnie, or so Arnie said, going to Syd's defence when he was questioned about whether he had slept the afternoon away. George duly packed the boot.

'Leave plenty of room for Syd's gear,' I quipped, which amused Arnie and George but Syd less so.

We were soon onto the road and heading for the Chequers. George assumed the role of navigator, relegating Arnie and me to the back, which did not worry me at all. Whether I drove, sat in the front or in the back, I was equally content, although I did find that sitting and relaxing in the back made a welcome change from driving. Arnie, however, was not at ease at all. I could see him shifting his position and feel him tensing his muscles when Syd half-turned to join in the conversation or reinforce a point which he thought necessitated looking us in the eye. The most unusual mannerism Syd had, which really destroyed Arnie's confidence, was to exaggerate a backward and forward movement when overtaking. He would suddenly grip the steering wheel when he began to accelerate and pull himself forward to such an extent that his nose was nearly touching the steering wheel. He would then rock back into the seat, assuming a more normal driving posture before pulling himself upright again. Backwards and forwards he went, doing what looked like vertical press-ups, unconsciously urging the car forward and past the other vehicle. Once this had been accomplished he would settle comfortably back into his seat before he needed to overtake again. Even if a car was fifty yards in front of us, I could tell that Syd was considering overtaking it when his hands began to take a more positive grip on the steering wheel, showing the whites of his knuckles, and his shoulders began to twitch. Arnie's face displayed distinct anxiety at this manoeuvre, and he was not completely relaxed even when Syd was facing forward and not attempting to overtake another vehicle. It must be awful to be a poor passenger, I thought as I enjoyed the scenery and conversation, watching with some amusement the tell-tale expressions on Arnie's face.

Arnie was very pleased when we reached the car park at the Chequers, breathing a sigh of relief as he stretched his legs. Without his hat, which was so much a part of his image, Syd did not look quite the part when he entered the pub. No one argued when George suggested that he should buy the first round. Although the room was fairly full, Syd sat in his customary place at a table by the window, which overlooked the car park. Arnie and I waited with George to help with the drinks. Although there was some room next to Syd, I nudged Arnie and nodded across to the other side of the room. He quickly picked up my intention of making an issue about the state of Syd's underwear and relayed the message to George. 'Bert will excel himself in this situation,' I said to Arnie.

I gave Syd his pint and went over to another table in the room which was small, intimate and in tradition with many village hostelries. Arnie and George soon followed, leaving Syd talking to the regulars on his side of the room and looking across at us from time to time with a sheepish grin on his face.

'What's the matter with those three?' asked one or two people.

'Don't know, really,' said Syd, trying not to show any embarrassment, for he had interpreted what we were up to very quickly. He could not really say anything, isolated as he was, and he knew very well that if he moved to our table we would promptly move to his. Most of the people in there were far too polite to ask why we sat apart; and the people we knew who came in later merely looked at us quizzically before becoming involved in the conversation.

Then the moment we had been waiting for arrived. Bert, not waiting for a break in the conversation, demanded to know if we had fallen out with Syd. We carried on talking as if we had not heard him. Then George looked up casually and, in a surprised voice, said, 'Ah, Bert there you are.' He took three or four rapid sniffs of the atmosphere before asking Bert if the peculiar smell in the room was anything to do with a blocked drain. Bert charged round the room like some rampant bloodhound. He would not stand any criticism of the way he ran the pub, kept it or looked after the beer. Occasionally, just for pure devilment, I would pick up my glass, hold it up to the light and suggest to Arnie and George that the beer might be a little cloudy, at a time when I knew Bert would be listening. This would prompt Bert to repeat after every inspection, 'I can't see it, can you?' to any customer who was near. 'Must be a dirty glass, then,' Arnie and George would suggest, supporting my original statement. 'My glasses are never dirty!' Bert would shout, going red in the face with outrage. 'Oh, never mind, I'll drink it anyway, stop fussing,' I would say, after we had extracted enough sport from the situation.

'I can't smell anything,' Bert repeated, after sniffing every corner of the room. 'Can you smell anything?' he asked everyone, hoping for reassurance.

By this time Syd was half-lying, half-leaning on the bench seat behind the table. He was holding his forehead and wiping his eyes, at the same time ordering Bert not to listen to us any more. Suddenly Bert twigged.

'Is the smell they are on about anything to do with you?' he asked.

'Come on, Sydney, tell Uncle Bert about your day,' Arnie, George and I chorused.

By this time the whole room was intrigued and it went unusually quiet. Syd realised he was cornered. He revealed the events of the day which amused everyone to varying degrees, but his parting shot of how he was going to ask his wife to remove the map of Ireland he had printed on his Y-fronts, rendered everyone, including us three who, after all, knew the story pretty well, virtually helpless.

Syd had the last laugh as he did on many occasions: several people bought him drinks, claiming that he was better entertainment than the cinema or television, which left the three of us to buy our own. I made Arnie feel really uncomfortable when I pointed to Syd, who was revelling in the adulation of his audience, and remarked, 'He has the task of driving us home,' at the same time holding an imaginary steering wheel and moving backwards and forwards in imitation of Syd overtaking.

Parts of Syd's story were repeated time and time again before the end of the evening, mostly by popular request. Eventually we left to face Syd driving us home, which was not quite as alarming as we had feared, probably because of the tranquillising effects of the evening.

CHAPTER FIFTEEN

'I'll be joining you on the Derwent tomorrow,' Wim informed us during a lull in one of the many arguments which occurred during the Friday evening ritual of dominoes.

'Wonderful,' we all agreed, before our voices were again raised in frustration and anguish as we tried simultaneously to prove some point in the game.

I think dominoes, particularly the game called 'fives and threes', provokes more hysteria from grown men than any other pub game — or any game at all, for that matter. The stakes are insignificant, but the pride in winning, or the dishonour of losing, seem to inflame the passions of the meekest of men. How two pairs of players, placing dominoes on a table and calculating how many times five and three divide into the sum of the spots on the two exposed ends, can manifest such apparently childish behaviour, will only be understood by those who play the game. The majority of the arguments come from the two players who are supposedly on the same side. The idea is for one player to indicate to his partner by his method of play what his hand contains and, by manipulation of the dominoes, a good player can help his partner to extract the maximum number of points from a given situation, or vice versa. Obviously, in a good domino school, the opposition are well-educated players, too, and they will try to thwart this scheme in order to develop their own strategy. Occasionally one of the partners plays a poor domino, either through misreading or misunderstanding his partner's intentions or, as sometimes happens, because he has only one domino which will match one of the ends, leaving him no alternative but to follow suit. This is followed by groans of dismay, and the withering looks which pass between the warriors of the domino board are enough to frighten all but the most fearless of men. All this is aided and abetted by the well-informed observers, who are all self-confessed experts of the game and quite willing to help the outbreak of civil war. 'I wouldn't have played that domino, either,' one spectator may whisper into the ear of a player who has just challenged his partner's wisdom in playing a certain domino. Other spectators will quietly 'tut tut' or shake their heads in an exaggerated display of disbelief, all of which adds to the gladiatorial atmosphere of a friendly traditional game, and all for the sake of threepence.

The fiercest and most prolonged argument, and the one in which everyone can join, occurs when all four players have forgotten whose drop it is. Each player in turn should play the first domino. After this, going clockwise round the table, each player takes his turn, providing he has a domino with the corresponding number of spots to match those at either end of the line as it is built up during the game. The drop, or the first domino played, is very significant for the way his partner or the opposition plays and acts as an indicator to a good, poor or indifferent hand. How, then, if everyone is playing according to the drop, can the person who actually dropped be forgotten once that particular hand is finished?

To a total stranger, the comments which follow this phenomenon must seem quite unbelievable. George, on these occasions, was always the first to announce in his most forth-right manner that he certainly did not drop but knew who did. Funnily enough, he would never say who it was, which at once sowed the seed of doubt in our minds. Arnie always tried to think things through, ponderously recapping on each stage of play before finally coming to the conclusion that he had not got a clue. Wim also adopted the scientific approach, but after several minutes of careful examination of the facts would produce a sequence of events from a game played some thirty minutes earlier, much to the amusement of the spectators. Wim was at this time a prospective parliamentary candidate for Ilkeston and listed dominoes as one of his hobbies. He did not reach Parliament, which was probably just as well, because his powers of deduction suggested to me that a ministerial post in the Department of Education and Science was highly likely.

During a break from the serious business of trying to deprive people of threepence, we all agreed how pleasing it would be to see Wim on the river for the first time. After all, his business commitments and weekends in pursuit of salmon and sea-trout on the Esk near Carlisle left little time for a spot of brownie fishing. He turned down our offer of a lift, explaining that it would take him the morning to cut his lawns after many days of neglect.

He had begun fishing when he was twelve on the river Ecclesbourne which flows from the limestone-quarried town of Wirksworth, joining the river Derwent about a hundred yards above the Bridge Inn at Duffield, the place where George, Arnie and I had made our first tentative efforts at fly fishing. Although I did not know the stretch of river above the town where Wim fished, I did know the Ecclesbourne, or at least the lower reaches just below Duffield, from my cricketing days. The river flows through the town, passing the cricket ground and crossing a field before entering the larger river. There was something about that cricket ground which affected me. The setting was quite charming, nestling beneath well-wooded hills. The perimeter of the ground was circled with white posts and rails to keep inquisitive cows or young bullocks at bay. The red-brick pavilion, with its white-painted front, stood high, with the changing rooms over the ground floor which housed the gang mowers, wicket mower, and numerous tins for holding the white-wash and brushes used for marking out the lines on the wicket. Old bats, broken stumps and bristleless brushes lay forgotten in the dust and grass of the groundsman's domain.

160

In sharp contrast to the brick pavilion, the tea hut on the other side of the ground was made of wood which was almost black from the countless gallons of creosote it must have received over the years.

Always, when I arrived there, the ground was well manicured. The outfield was a lush dark green and mown in circles, contrasting well with the short grass of the actual square with its alternating light and dark green swathes, and the brown strip devoid of grass which signified the wicket for the day.

How long shall I last at the crease today? I remember contemplating while climbing the steep steps to the dressing room which was clearly marked for the visitors.

'Are you going to score a run this year?' asked one of the players, much to the amusement of the others.

'Another walk down the river, is it?' questioned another. As an opening batsman it was my job to score runs. Duffield became a nightmare for me. I cannot recall scoring a single run there, and many times I suffered the indignity of being out first ball. Over the years I must have spent many solitary hours walking from the ground to the Ecclesbourne and along its banks. I would follow the river, watching the stickles, eddies and pools and listening to the song of the birds punctuated by the distinct crack of willow on leather coming from my more successful team-mates. By the time I had made my way to the Derwent, along its banks and across the field back to the ground, it was usually and conveniently time for the tea-interval; I never realised how important those two rivers were to become.

Wim fished the river Ecclesbourne above the town, as a guest of one of the members of the club which bore the name of the river which was leased from the Strutt Estate. He said how good the fishing was, but it was difficult for me to imagine how fish survived in such a small river compared with the relatively wide expanses of the Derwent.

It was mid-afternoon the following day when Wim finally

161

arrived on the river, although I did not recognise him immediately. I was fishing some way below the car park when I noticed a stranger walking slowly down the river towards me. Although he was some distance away, I could see that the figure was wearing waders, a deer-stalker type hat and looked like a fisherman, but instead of carrying a rod, bag and net he held a tall, heavy wading stick.

'Anything doing, Smithy?' I heard, when the man came within earshot. The voice made me jump, and it was still echoing across the valley when I recognised its owner as Wim. I was quite surprised that he should be the figure strolling so nonchalantly down the river. It was the first time I had seen him in anything other than a suit or everyday clothes, and it was a dramatic change, even at a distance. I left the river and joined him on the bank, feeling very pleased to see him.

He commented on the day and the pleasant surroundings, and asked whether I was having any success or not. 'How many fields are there before I reach the boundary of our fishing?' he enquired.

My reply was somewhat vague as I gazed at his attire. I was bemused by his waders which were wrinkled about his legs in a good imitation of two old, deflated concertinas. He had dispensed with or lost the straps which should have been clipped to the tops of his waders and then attached to a belt or buttons at the waist, which would hold them up and keep them taut. They were covered in a variety of rubber patches of different colours and sizes. The visible part of the trousers between his coat and waders was also patched in places with a different colour, style and weave of material from the original. His coat, which must have been a well-loved, comfortable old sports jacket, was buttonless and held together more or less in the middle by a large, shiny safety pin. His hat was faded with age and well-worn, revealing parts of the stiffening which reinforced the peaks, and dotted with a number of mutilated flies. It was some time before I had

162

completely absorbed how a company director dressed for a day's fishing.

'Why aren't you fishing?' I asked. 'Where's your rod?'

'I am fishing,' he said, and explained that he had left his rod at his car and that he would see me later. I could not understand this at the time as he lazily wandered off.

The river was very active, with swirls, splashes and dimples of the eagerly feeding fish, which kept me occupied until it was time to meet the others for a drink and something to eat before we began the evening's fishing.

'I see Wim's arrived,' Arnie commented, on finding his car in the car park. 'Where is he fishing?'

'He isn't,' I said, and went on to tell them that I had met him wandering down the river with nothing but a long wading stick. They could not understand this any more than I could. We were just finishing our refreshments when we saw a lone figure wading up the river.

'That's Wim,' George exclaimed. 'What is he doing?'

We watched him intently as he waded the river. Across, up and back he went, prodding and testing the depth with his stick. He meticulously searched and probed the bed of the river amongst the rocks and in the stickles, pausing and watching for a while before moving on. It suddenly occurred to me, when I thought of his earlier comment, that he was fishing after all, even without a rod. He was prepared to analyse the depth of water, the flow and how best to approach the various stretches of river. I realised while I was watching Wim that his approach to fishing in unfamiliar surroundings was completely different from ours. We had originally looked at the water to check where the boundaries were and had superficially observed likely places where trout would feed, but once our first season started and fish began to show, we seldom ventured away from the first place we had found, which we came to regard as the only place for us to be. We had tested and come to know the depth of the river in our self-restricted areas by months of trial and error, by seeing how far the water progressed towards the tops of our waders. Wim was gaining knowledge of the whole of the river bed in a controlled and scientific manner, which indicated to me that he was a truly experienced fisherman. I could see him making mental notes of landmarks, currents and depths and soon began to realise with some embarrassment that he already knew far more about the river in the few hours that he had been there than I did in the months I had been fishing.

'How can he walk past all those fish just asking to be caught?' questioned George, looking on in disbelief.

'I'm sure he knows where they are for the future,' said Arnie, slowly beginning to realise what he was doing and why.

Wim left the water when he saw us and joined us for a while before telling us that he was going to walk the rest of the river.

'Aren't you taking a rod with you?' asked George.

'Not just yet,' he said emphatically.

'Whyever not, with all those fish rising?'

'It's called self-discipline,' said Wim. 'I know very well that if I take a rod with me I'll be tempted to cast over some of the fish and that isn't the way I begin fishing unfamiliar territory. It may be peculiar to me but I need to know the extent of the water, the various depths, currents and characteristics of the bed before I can settle and begin to cast a fly seriously.' As soon as he had gone George, Arnie and Syd commented on his appearance and were as bemused as I was by what they saw.

Arnie suggested that Wim paddling about in the river would stop many fish rising, so we chose to fish below the car park during the evening and did not see Wim again until we arrived back at the car. He was casting over some fish which were rising in the stretch just above the car park. Effortlessly he lifted the line off the water before returning it delicately, presenting the fly beautifully over a rising fish.

'Just look at that,' I said. We watched and could see that Wim's skill, after many years of experience, made casting look easy and effortless and painted a picture of graceful charm. This was enhanced for me when I looked at the angles the line was making with the bank and the river; they were less acute than usual and altered by the fact that he fished left-handed. How compatible with nature, I thought as I compared his movements with those of the quiet, controlled flight of the birds or the flies and the apparent controlled ease with which a mallard or moorhen combats the currents.

'How long have you been fishing there?' asked George, after we had changed and were ready to leave.

'Oh, about half an hour,' came the reply. 'I'll just give it another ten minutes and then I'll meet you in the Chequers, where I hope a pint will be waiting for me.'

Sure enough, shortly after we arrived Wim joined us. 'Where's my pint, then?' we could hear coming from behind the screen which separated the back room where we were sitting from the bar area. The bar at the Chequers was a peculiar arrangement and I should imagine quite unique. It was nothing more than an extra-wide shelf, supported underneath by other smaller shelves which held the clean glasses. It was open to the public, standing as it did in the passage-way which led from the back door to the front room. The till was a single drawer located beneath the wider shelf and was locked with a single nail which penetrated the serving area directly above the drawer and lodged against one of its partitions. The nail was shiny, smooth and polished after years of constant use and was bent by the countless times the partition had bumped against it when the drawer was inadvertently pulled while it was still in the locked position. The beer was served from large enamel jugs drawn straight from the barrels in the cellar, which were clearly visible through an open door at the side of the bar. This arrangement dispensed with the need for pumps and taps which are standard equipment in most public houses.

The Chequers Inn at Stanton-by-Dale.

'Your pint's here, Wim,' called Bert over the hubbub of noise. 'I'll look after you even if they won't,' he added, once again trying to become part of the act. I was amazed, when Wim walked in to join us, to see that he was still dressed in the same sports jacket and trousers and sported the same faded hat. We had changed, as we always did, from our fishing gear into something more respectable for our pint at the end of the day. Wim obviously thought quite differently as he sat down and immediately began to fiddle with one of the patches in his trousers. This in itself would not have mattered, but the one he chose was in the gusset immediately below his zip. Syd began to chuckle and I could see Arnie and George going hot under the collar as he proceeded absent-mindedly to break the stitching and poke his finger through the hole. I felt a little embarrassed when I saw other people looking, intrigued at what Wim was doing, deliberately trying to avert their gaze before they were compelled to look again to see if any progress had been made.

'Quite a nice stretch of water,' he commented while finishing off his pint, which at least put an end to his fiddling, and he ordered another round quite unperturbed about his appearance. We did not say a word about this until we were in the car on our way to George's where Syd had left his car. 'I couldn't walk into a public place looking like that,' chuckled Syd, which was the thought which must have been going through all our minds.

'I'll tell you one thing,' I said. 'Despite his appearance, his attitude to fishing and his approach to it are far superior to ours. He has spent only a few hours with us and has learned far more about the river than we have in the months we have been fishing there, even though he only cast a fly for about an hour.'

'Yes, he is quite a character,' volunteered George as he got out of the car to remove the tackle from the boot.

CHAPTER SIXTEEN

We continued to enjoy our fishing throughout that year, with varying degrees of success. On some days we caught several fish between us, while on others the river proved to be at its most possessive and refused to give up anything apart from its solitude, beauty and tranquil charm. I accepted quite easily that even though I expected to catch a fish at some time during every visit there would be some days when I would not. Even on the most stubborn days, I never lost the thrill of anticipation when I was down by the river casting a fly over a rising fish. For me it was very similar to a game of cricket. Some games we won, some we lost and some we drew and, at a personal level, sometimes I did well while at other times I failed. When fishing, the river became my opposition; sometimes I considered I had won, sometimes I knew I had lost, but on many occasions, while I was changing at the end of the day and looking at the river sweeping peacefully through the hills, I thought that the contest had been an honourable draw. I felt that a bond had built up between me and the river. At the end of a particularly good day I gave it a knowing look, thinking I had mastered its idiosyncrasies. At the end of a less productive day I gazed ruefully at its waters and wondered what might have been, and I reverently acknowledged it when I thought the day was even. I was sure that my thoughts were reciprocated when I gave it a final departing look as I drove from the river to join the road and begin the journey back to civilisation.

August is a notoriously difficult month for fishing, when all the fish seem to be preoccupied with feeding on the tiny reed smuts which hatch in their thousands and appear on the river. They are difficult to imitate because of their size, and even the smallest Black Gnats look huge on the water beside the almost invisible black specks. It very often appeared to me, as I watched a feeding fish, that he was rising and feeding on nothing at all, until my eyes adjusted and focused on these tiny dots on the water's surface. More often than not, during the day, the sun was high and bright and must have reflected my line and the knots on the leader and warned many fish of an unnatural presence. They were quiet, lazy days which suited Syd's leisurely approach to the sport quite admirably. He enjoyed his pipe, his sleep and a not too serious amble and fish down the river and would always stop and talk to anyone who was prepared to pass the time of day with him. For George, Arnie, Wim when he joined us and me, it was more of an uneven, masochistic contest we became involved in when we tried to deceive a fish in the most difficult conditions, although one day I did give up the battle temporarily when I came across George towards the top of our stretch of river.

'How are you doing?' he called from the river.

'I'm finding these conditions very difficult as usual,' I replied, while he lethargically made his way from the river, suggesting to me that he welcomed a break from his efforts. We sat for a while, gratefully contemplating, despite the inconsiderate fish, how lucky we were to have been accepted into a fishing club which provided such a good stretch of water and in such a pleasing setting.

'Where are you going now?' he asked, after we had rested for a while.

'I'm going to fish, or at least walk as far as the boundary.'

'Do you mind if I join you?' George asked.

'Not at all,' I replied, replacing my bag, which seemed unusually heavy, on my shoulder.

We walked along a high bank looking down into the river before turning a corner where we could see the limit of our water two fields away, marked by a farmhouse and the Square and Compass Inn, which stood on the roadside just beyond the bridge that crossed the Derwent. I could see a well-trodden footpath leading through the fields and through the narrow gaps in the stone walls, which allowed the walkers to pass through but were narrow enough to retain the cattle which grazed in the fields. It was a very hot, sticky day; even the effort of walking seemed arduous. I gazed across at the inn and saw the symbol of a square and a compass depicted in white-painted tiles on its otherwise dark grey roof. George must have been reading my thoughts as I visualised a cool pint, at the same time asking him what time it was.

'We'll just make it,' he said, taking off his bag and net and placing them with his rod which he had concealed in the long grass at the side of the wall. It had mine for company in next to no time. I do not know whether it was the thought of a pint or our new freedom of movement in our unladen state, but the walk across the fields seemed relatively easy. The sign on the roof grew larger and larger as we made rapid progress along the path and through the gaps in the walls.

'I'm not going to tell them, are you?' enquired George in a sheepish manner.

'Not likely,' I replied, knowing at once that he was thinking of Syd and Arnie somewhere down the river, suffering from heat and fatigue and lacking our opportunity for a quick pint of cooling beer. 'Can we go in wearing waders?' I asked.

George was tripping over the step in a manner which suggested that he had been in the deserts of Africa for months on end. 'Just watch me,' he said, striding towards the bar in his usual determined manner, sounding like an army on a parade ground as his studs made contact with the tiled floor. The noise of my studs was drowned by George asking for two pints from the landlord, who looked pleased to see us and seemed very grateful for our custom. George smiled

170

before removing the top three inches of beer from his pint glass, which he followed with a long sigh of pleasure.

'Do you know, I feel really guilty,' I said as I grasped the cool drink.

'So do I,' he said, trying to impose an expression of mock guilt on his very contented countenance. We stayed for another pint, vowing not to tell Arnie and Syd about our clandestine visit. 'Mind you, Syd did the same to us, don't forget,' George remarked, which somehow made him feel much better and helped to ease his conscience. Every time the door opened we looked round furtively to see who was coming in, in case we were caught in the act; it reminded me of the times when I used to take the odd pint or two after playing cricket, before I had reached the age for a legal drink.

We found the walk back to pick up the rods and bags much less arduous, and I even detected a jauntiness in George's step which had not been there before, and a smile of satisfaction on his face. This had something to do with the thought that we had stolen a couple of pints while Arnie and Syd were having to refresh themselves with tea or coffee, judging by his comments about how sorry he felt that they had not been able to join us. 'Mind you, they would have refused our invitation anyway, even if we had asked them,' I maintained in an equally sarcastic manner.

'I'm really ready for a pint,' Arnie gasped while he was taking off his waders at the end of the day's fishing.

'I couldn't agree with you more,' I said. 'It's been a very hot, sticky day and I'm beginning to feel the effects of dehydration. How about you?' I asked George who was packing the boot and exaggeratedly making sure that everything was in its place, which meant that he could keep his sheepishly smiling face well hidden.

'I might just manage one,' he said, not daring to turn round.

'I was very tempted to nip off for one at dinner time,' chimed in Syd in a voice whose huskiness was meant to convince us that he was suffering from moisture loss and feeling very parched.

'Disgusting thought,' I said, trying to instil horror into my voice at the thought of such a suggestion. 'You wouldn't have left us sweating it out in the heat of the day, while you satisfied your thirst with a pint, no doubt chuckling when you thought about us. You wouldn't have enjoyed a pint anyway,' I said. 'Your conscience and feelings of guilt when you thought of us would have made it impossible for you to swallow it.'

George collapsed into the boot at this point, unable to control himself any longer. I could not contain myself either, and joined George in hysterical laughter. It was even worse when I saw Arnie's face: he was scowling with indignation, sending furrows across his forehead.

'Whatever is the matter with those two?' Syd asked Arnie.

'Don't you know? Don't you know?' he replied heatedly. 'They've been to the pub for a pint.'

'So much for friends,' said Syd, when the truth of what George and I had done began to dawn.

'Just a minute, I can remember someone sitting enjoying a pint while we were fishing, *and* keeping us waiting,' remarked George, reminding Syd of his lunchtime drink with Fred as he packed everything neatly away.

Wim joined us at the Chequers later in the evening and immediately enquired about how the day had progressed.

'Much the same as usual,' I said, describing the smutting habits of the fish.

'How do you know? You've spent most of the day in the Square and Compass,' interrupted Arnie, still smarting over our lunchtime truancy and looking pointedly at Wim for sympathetic words of support.

'No gentleman would do such a thing,' said Wim, acting as both judge and jury.

'I'm pleased you wouldn't,' said Arnie, obviously encouraged by these comments.

'Oh, I would quite happily, and enjoy every minute of it,' laughed Wim. 'I did say a *gentleman* wouldn't do such a thing.

'I've been thinking, getting back to more serious matters, that we are fishing at the wrong time of the day,' he went on. 'We are leaving the river just when many of the fish are beginning to feed on the larger flies on the surface for the first time at the latter end of the day, when the smuts are less abundant. In my experience, many rivers fish much better and are more productive in the hour or so before dusk.' He went on to say that he had often seen rivers come alive in the late evening, which was more or less the time when we were travelling back, to arrive at the Chequers early enough for a pint.

'What do you suggest we do?' George asked tentatively, showing some alarm at the prospect of missing the company and repartee, not to mention the well-earned pint, all of which he considered a necessary and satisfactory conclusion to his day.

'Why not try Friday evening?' Wim proposed.

'This place would fall down,' quipped Arnie before agreeing that it was a good idea.

'We could fish until dusk and then call at the Square and Compass,' Wim went on.

'What about the dominoes?' questioned George, still slightly taken aback at Wim's suggestion.

'It will only be for the odd Friday before the nights really begin to draw in,' I said, agreeing with Arnie that it sounded like a good suggestion and committing Syd to show approval.

'Next Friday, then, if the weather's fine,' we all agreed, before arranging to meet in Wim's factory car park, where Syd would leave his car and travel with Wim.

* * *

'It seems funny not shuffling the ivories tonight,' George

173

said as we set out the following Friday. He sounded almost apologetic, as if the dominoes would be offended. Arnie and I agreed that to be on the river in the mellowing light of a summer evening held an overwhelming fascination which more than compensated for missing a game of dominoes.

'What could be better than this?' Arnie asked George when we stood by the river.

'Nothing at all,' conceded George. He looked at the water and inhaled the fresh, clean air, commenting on the lengthening shadows which would help to diffuse and camouflage our lines. 'We must be rather silly sitting in a smoke-filled room getting agitated over a game, when we have all this.'

I'm pleased you're beginning to see things in perspective,' I said and suggested that breaking routines sometimes has the effect of giving certain people a sense of insecurity.

Arnie, too, felt that a break in our routine might work to our advantage. 'Just think,' he said thoughtfully, 'all those fish won't be expecting us tonight, which will make it much easier for us to catch them. They know by now that we only appear on Saturdays, which means that they'll be off their guard until about ten o'clock tomorrow morning.'

'I wish I was so convinced about the fishes' ability to think and apply logic,' I said, 'although I must admit that it often seems like that.'

'You aren't wearing that, are you?' Syd asked when I donned my waterproof fishing coat.

'It might be wise. I know it's hot and sunny now, but storms have been forecast for later on.'

'Rubbish,' said Wim, launching into a tirade against weather forecasters who were far from being his favourite people, lacking, he said, in skill, knowledge and good manners. 'What other type of person can stand up and tell millions of people a deliberate lie on one day, and then refuse to apologise the following day before fabricating the truth once again?' he burst out in an agitated crescendo.

'Quite right,' muttered the others.

'You believe what you like,' I said, keeping my coat in place and setting off down the river.

'You'll be far too hot,' commented Syd, amid murmurings of agreement from George and Arnie.

It was becoming a matter of principle now that I should keep my coat on, even though it was uncomfortably hot. The effect it had while I walked down the river was bad enough, but casting was almost torture: I could feel hot air rising from inside my coat and the perspiration increased with every move. It's a good thing it isn't tight, I thought, smiling to myself at my mental image of a fisherman floating up and over the hills like some human hot air balloon.

The more the evening wore on, the more the fish began to rise, just as Wim had predicted. It *is* a good time to be on the river, I thought, as I watched hundreds of female flies dancing and hopping over the water, laying their eggs. They left tiny rings where they had temporarily alighted on the water before moving to the next selected place. Hundreds, maybe thousands, maybe millions of eggs must have been descending to the bed of the river to seek shelter amongst the stones and pebbles. Other flies were floating down, lying flat and motionless on the surface with their wings spread out, their duty done, while others twitched occasionally with the last gasps of their short but hectic lives. I could see fish hungrily feeding on these corpses which were by now a predominant feature on the water. That's what a spent or spinner pattern of fly looks like, I thought to myself, relating this new experience to the relevant information about the life cycle of a fly which I could recall from the books I had read or from entomological conversations.

A distant, muted rumble in the hills distracted me. I looked along the valley in the general direction of the muffled noise. In the distance the clear, dark blue sky of the late summer evening ended abruptly in a heaving mass of swirling cloud. The leading edges were white and rounded, ballooning high into the sky, and appeared to be layered in both depth and height. These clouds preceded the dense, ominous-looking rain clouds, which marched slowly along the valley, spurred on by the intermittent flashes of darting light streaking earthward, and a fanfare of booms and rumbles which echoed round the quickly disappearing valley. I am experiencing a natural performance of what Beethoven created musically in the fourth movement of his Sixth Symphony, I thought, feeling honoured to be part of the audience as I listened and watched.

It was very still and noticeably quiet between these bursts of noise. The birds had stopped singing, the fish were not rising and the leaves on the trees and the grasses and flowers were motionless, as if they were standing to attention, eager to show respect for the approach of a superior natural force.

I was halfway to the car before the first cold, heavy spots of rain began to fall and the breeze began to pick up. The water became speckled and I could hear it start to chatter with the raindrops which left rings radiating from the points of impact. The leaves nodded and bowed under the weight of the rain and the grasses and flowers waved and rustled in the increasing wind, all applauding in their way the arrival of the awesome presence. By the time I had reached the car the rain was pouring down vertically, obliterating the hills and making the river hiss and steam. It ran off my coat and hat in continuous rivulets. I wondered where the others were, feeling very grateful for the protection of my coat.

'Come and shelter under here,' I could hear coming from the small railway bridge which spanned the track just beyond the car park. I walked over and found Syd, Arnie and George dodging the drops leaking through from above. They looked cold and miserable, but surprisingly were only slightly damp.

'Were you near the car when the storm broke?' I asked.

'Fortunately, yes,' they replied although George, who was furthest away, told me that he had run for cover as soon as he heard the first rumble in the hills.

'You can't have done much fishing, then,' I suggested.

'Fancy coming all this way to fish the river and ending up sitting under a railway bridge.' I could not resist a comment about the accuracy of the weather forecasts and my high regard for the men who delivered them.

'I suppose you are perfectly dry and warm,' sneered Syd.

'Of course I am,' I said in a deliberately smug manner, although I could still feel the earlier effects of the heat from my coat which had made my shirt uncomfortably moist in places.

'I wonder where Wim is,' said Arnie, after we had been sheltering for some time. 'I hope he's all right.'

'No doubt he'll appear soon,' I said, moving from under the bridge to look down the valley where I could see horizontal light breaks in the otherwise dark and gloomy sky.

Sure enough, as soon as the rain eased a little Wim appeared. He was wet through. The water shone on his shirt and on his trousers where they were visible above his waders. What hair he had lay in heavy water-logged strands down his neck, releasing trickles of water which disappeared below the collar of his open shirt.

'Why didn't you shelter?' asked George, concerned.

'I was so interested in casting to a fish which was being annoyingly elusive that I was fairly wet before I realised it. When I did find shelter I realised that I had dropped my landing net somewhere and had to search for it,' explained Wim, blowing away spots of water which were dripping off the end of his nose.

When the worst seemed to be over, we decided that the best thing to do was to change and seek the warmth of the Square and Compass. Quickly we changed into dry clothes, grateful to have the tree in the car park which provided at least some shelter, and although it felt temporarily uncomfortable walking on the wet grass while we changed into our socks and shoes, we were soon feeling warmer and dry. Apart from Wim, we all now had coats on to protect us from another heavy burst of rain. Wim was messing about

177

in his car, which seemed to annoy George who was thinking about Wim's welfare.

'Aren't you going to change?' he asked, busily looking after the boot of my car. 'You'll catch pneumonia if you aren't careful.'

'Yes, now that everything's ready,' came the reply. Within seconds Wim threw everything off and was standing stark naked under the tree with the rain dripping from every appendage. It was running off his nose, off his chin and off his elbows. I could hear Syd and Arnie, who were by now comfortable in the back of the car, laughing at this spectacle. George looked horrified.

'There's some excess flesh there, I said to George, pointing to places which wobbled as Wim vigorously towelled himself down. George finally relieved his embarrassment with the comment, 'Well, Wim, to say you are a ladies' man, I can't see what they see in you,' pointedly referring to the lowest prolongation before his toes.

'I bet they don't come back for second helpings!' Syd shouted from the car.

'I can't say that I'm all that impressed, are you, Arnie?' I asked.

'Not really. Mind you, it *is* cold and his system's had a bit of a shock.'

Wim held the towel in front of himself, pretending to be embarrassed by the comments before putting on a dry shirt and another pair of well patched but dry trousers.

'I say, Wim, do you buy your trousers like that?' I said, pointing to the patches which were almost in the identical places of those on the pair he had just removed.

'Stop the cheek, Smithy, and go and buy a round, I'm nearly ready,' he retorted. I obeyed his command and drove round to the Square and Compass through more rain. The car park was awash with the effects of the storm.

'What a beautiful sight,' whispered Arnie as he felt the

warmth of the room and saw the cheerful flames from a coal fire which was burning brightly in the grate.

'I wouldn't have thought that would be necessary when we began fishing,' Syd commented to George, equally pleased to see the firelight flickering.

'There's a table there,' I said, pointing across the room. 'Go and commandeer it while I order the first round.'

'It's nice to see you on such a dismal evening,' greeted the landlord, which made a welcome change from Bert's rendering of 'The Fishermen of England'. I carefully carried over five pints on a tray and just as carefully placed them on the table. It would be sheer sacrilege to spill any, and I knew from past experience that they would be intently watching me to make the most of any incompetence.

'There you are, I didn't spill a drop,' I said, and pointed out that I could now settle down with an easy conscience and critically watch their performances.

'I feel much better now,' said George, shaking his shoulders in an exaggerated shiver.

'Yes, he must be a shrewd landlord,' we all agreed, feeling the warm glow of the open fire.

Wim walked in a little later, carrying his socks in one hand and a pair of shoes in the other. I half rose to see what he was wearing on his feet which I discovered, after a second glance, were bare. He walked towards the bar, looking round to see where we were sitting before Syd called, 'Over here, Wim.' The room went gradually quiet and the conversation became more stilted as eyes followed other people's gazes, coming to rest in disbelief on Wim's bare feet. They then looked back in the direction of the door and followed a set of wet footprints which were clearly marked on the red quarry-tiled floor. By the time Wim had reached the centre of the room there was a hushed silence as everyone stared, transfixed by the sight of ten toes and a track of wet footmarks. At this point Wim paused and folded his arms, still holding his shoes and socks, across his chest.

'Well, gentlemen,' he said, 'I'm pleased to be in a quiet and orderly house and if by any slight chance I've had something to do with that I can assure you that I don't make a habit of walking in like this, but on this occasion the circumstances demanded it.'

'Well said,' I remarked from the table in our corner and began to applaud Wim's bold statement; many more joined in and it certainly relieved the awkward silence. The pub was soon back to normal, a hubbub of intense political arguments, laughter, the rattle of dominoes being shuffled and the thud of darts hitting the board.

Wim followed George's gaze which was fixed intently on a game of dominoes at the next table. 'Have you missed your game?' he said, concentrating more on the surroundings now that he was fully clothed.

'I suppose I have a little, but I would not have missed tonight for anything, and it's beautiful sitting by this lovely open fire. Come on, let's have another pint.'

This little phrase was repeated three more times before we left at about a quarter to twelve.

'A piece of toast done on those embers would go down very well,' I said, just as we were leaving. 'I'm beginning to feel a little pang or two of hunger.'

'I'm starving,' chorused Arnie and Syd.

'I didn't like to mention it,' added George.

'That's easily remedied. Fish and chips will round off a good evening. Follow me,' ordered Wim, 'I know just the place,' striding out of the room like the Pied Piper.

We travelled along the lanes through Winster, turning off to Middleton-by-Wirksworth and on to Wirksworth itself. Wim pulled up at a shop in the centre of the town and was soon inside ordering fish and chips, with Syd almost at his shoulder.

'What do you want? I'll get ours,' George offered. 'Fish or pie?'

'Oh, fish will do very well,' agreed Arnie and I, thanking

George for the waiter service. Fortunately, at this late hour the shop was relatively empty, so we did not have long to wait. I do not know whether it was the effects of the fresh air, the beer, which always acted like a good aperitif, or the hour, but I have never tasted such delicious fish and chips. The chips were dry and hot, the batter on the fish was crisp and crunchy and the flesh inside was as white as driven snow.

'Come on,' said Wim while we were disposing of the empty papers into a well-sited bin, 'I feel like a nightcap now.'

'Where on earth shall we get a drink at this time of night, it's gone midnight?' I asked.

'My office,' he said, giving me a knowing look.

Syd sank into the back of my car, quite content and very relaxed.

'What's the matter, don't you like Wim's driving?' I asked. It was some time before he realised he had been Wim's passenger until we stopped. He chuckled merrily, saying that we were all going to the same place so it would not really matter that he was in the wrong car, and he was sure that Wim would not be offended. I had three very docile passengers for company on the way back, although Syd did liven things up a little when he asked who had been planting roses in the grass verges at the side of the road.

'What roses?' I asked.

'Those,' he said, pointing to the red reflector discs which marked the sharp corners and bends on the country lanes.

'Are you sure you want another drink?' Arnie asked.

'Of course I do,' Syd replied, sinking further into the seat and tilting his hat over his eyes.

Soon we were sitting in Wim's office, reclining in the easy chairs and watching him open one of the drawers of a steel filing cabinet which contained numerous bottles.

'Scotch all round, I think,' he said, making a selection from the bottles.

'Just a minute,' I said, standing to attention with my glass

181

poised in a ceremonious manner. 'Before we have a drink I would like you to raise your glasses, while I propose a toast.'

'Who on earth to?' asked George.

'To Wim, our weatherman,' I replied.

'To Wim, our weatherman!' they laughingly chorused.

'All right, all right, they have to be right at least once,' conceded Wim, offering us another tot.

We were a captive audience as Wim began to reminisce about some of his fishing experiences. Enthralled, we listened as he described the days he had spent fishing for salmon on the Esk in Cumbria and the nights he had spent fishing for sea-trout on the same river. He could remember individual contests he had had with a fish and graphically described how many times it had run up and down the river, how he had landed it and what fly he had used, as though it had only happened yesterday. During a brief pause I glanced at my watch, which showed the time to be half past two.

'Gentlemen,' I said, 'it's now two-thirty and, reluctant as I feel to leave such company, unless we have some sleep we shall never be up in time to visit the river later on this morning.'

CHAPTER SEVENTEEN

Our journey to the river that Saturday was rather a quiet affair. We chose the country lanes to avoid the noise and bustle of the busy towns and the volume of traffic on the main roads. Even Syd was unusually subdued and Arnie was almost as relaxed as he had been the previous evening.

'It's a good job I'm alert,' I said, pointing out the reflectors which Syd had thought were roses, which did provoke one of his familiar chuckles.

'Do you fancy some chips?' George asked as we passed through Wirksworth.

'That's the last thing I want,' groaned Arnie, upset at the mention of food.

'Why, have you had a cooked breakfast?' Syd asked, which brought more groans from Arnie.

The road from Wirksworth climbed steeply past the massive limestone quarries and the buildings housing the machinery and plant which worked them. The trees, the verges and the road were white with dust from the crushers used to fragment the huge blocks dynamited from the hillside, leaving yawning holes, but also beautifully marked corrugated vertical walls, proudly showing the angular geometrical strata. The whole area was a labyrinth of covered ways for the miles of conveyor belts which carried the several sizes of graded limestone to the appropriate heaps; they stood silhouetted, cone-shaped and brilliantly white, against the dark green of the hillside and the trees on the other side of the valley. The road climbed on through the town of Middleton-by-Wirksworth where it narrowed, its width determined by the rows of cottages whose doors opened almost directly onto it, prohibiting any road-widening scheme. Then it plateaued out for a while, with a sheer drop on the right down to the well-known beauty spot of the Via Gellia and the road which ran through it, looking like a thread of cotton from this height.

The descent to the bottom of the valley was steep and dramatic, reassuringly guarded by substantially built stone walls. The route along the valley bottom was arched with trees which grew in the shallow stony soil and clung desperately to the rocks protruding from the steep slopes. The drive up the other side was more of a steady and gradual climb, which twisted and turned through an exposed and barren landscape of rough, fibrous pasture, segregated by miles and miles of weathered dry stone walls, with the occasional small stone building providing shelter for implements or cattle. The front of the car dipped under the heavy braking necessary to control its rate of descent down the steep gradient to the picturesque village of Winster with its small, quaint shops randomly placed among the rows of stone-built houses, and the arched Market House at the side of the main street.

Out in the country once more, we drove along a road overlooking a wooded valley. There was an old beamed engine house down there, a neglected relic of the once-thriving lead mining industry. I tried to imagine what it had looked like in its prime, with steam hissing from its valves and the gentle hum from well-oiled bearings. I wondered how many shafts and old workings were buried forever under the hills and what hardships the men had suffered in their isolated world. Another descent brought us to the village of Darley Dale where the bridge over the Derwent marked the upper limits of our fishing, past the Square and Compass immediately beyond and onto the main road which we briefly followed before turning through a gate and onto our welcome track.

'We might as well have stayed in Wim's office listening to

The village of Winster.

his accounts of his exploits,' muttered George, when we surveyed the Derwent. The water was 'high, wide and very filthy' from the effects of the storm the previous evening.

'I thought it might be like this,' said Arnie despondently, and indeed it seemed that fishing was impossible. I felt a sinking feeling in the pit of my stomach when I saw the water swirling behind the trees which usually stood high and dry on the bank, although I did not say anything for fear of adding to the gloom. Time and time again I looked at the river, hoping that it would suddenly drop and clear to reveal the pebbles on the bottom, the weeds and the boulders of its normal summer level.

'What are we going to do now?' asked George.

'We might as well have a walk in the fresh air,' I suggested.

'Upstream or downstream?' questioned Syd, who felt that the walk would do him good and clear his head.

'Let's walk up to the brook and see how much water is flowing into the Derwent from the hills,' said Arnie. 'I have never seen it running high.'

We replaced our shoes with waders to protect them from the wet grass and began to walk slowly and rather dejectedly up the river.

'It seems funny walking up here without a rod in my hand,' commented George, still upset at being deprived of a day's fishing.

Looking up at the trees, I saw how the leaves shone, looking refreshed after the rain had washed them and removed the dust and pollen which had settled on them from the grasses and flowers in the meadows. The taller grasses were bowing, still straining under the weight of the water they had collected, while the shorter, more sturdy varieties were holding individual droplets amongst their leaves, which glistened like diamonds when they caught and reflected the rays of the sun. I looked at the dark mounds of earth in the grass and traced the underground paths of the moles; it was easy to identify the work they had undertaken after the

186

storm, by the dry, granulated mounds standing out amongst the more depressed heaps where the soil had been fused together by the heavy rain. I pondered the fortunes of circumstance, thinking back to my first rod and Mr Hendy all those years ago; the chance meeting with Arnie some years later; the acquaintance and then the friendship we formed with Wim, Syd and Fred, and now the joy I found in observing nature brought about by a sudden storm.

I joined the others who were standing looking down at the cow-drink, where George usually entered the shallows and spent much of his time.

'I wouldn't like to wade in there today,' he said, looking at the swirling, darkened waters. 'There's a large boulder near this bank and even that is submerged.'

'Just a minute,' I said, walking down to the water's edge and pointing to some lines which had been etched in the sandy soil of the gently sloping bank. 'The water level must be falling quickly.'

'Why?' asked George with a sudden burst of optimism.

'Just look here,' I said, pointing to several steps which had been eroded into the bank. 'You can see the maximum height the river must have reached and how it has dropped in stages, by the ridges it has formed in the silt.'

'It must have held its level for some time and then dropped very quickly,' Arnie said as he inspected the distance between the first and the second steps. 'It's already dropped four more times after that, and must have held each level for a while before dropping further, although not so quickly,' he theorised, comparing the first wide band with the narrower bands of the lower steps.

'I wonder how long it has taken to fall to this level and how quickly it's falling now,' George remarked.

'We'll soon see,' I said, placing a stick at the water's edge and noting the time on my watch. 'We can check the rate of fall from this stick on our way back from the brook.'

The brook was running surprisingly clear, dispersing and

187

diluting the silty waters in an arc where it flowed into the main river.

'If this is running fairly clear and low, so should most of the other feeder streams by now,' suggested Arnie. George immediately wanted to go and check the marker and set off for the cow-drink at a cracking pace. He was first down by the river and was delighted to find the stick high and dry on the bank with the water flowing some distance away from it. He enthusiastically found another stick which he held horizontally across from the base of my marker and then another stick which he placed vertically in the bank at the water's edge. This made the third side of a triangle which gave him a fairly accurate reading of how much the water had dropped in vertical inches, rather than the distance down the sloping bank.

'Very scientific,' I said. 'That must be at least another inch in about half an hour,' checking my watch to see how long the walk to the brook and back had taken. 'We might be fishing in an hour or two at this rate of fall,' I suggested, looking at Arnie who was already surveying the water for the slightest hint of a rising fish.

'Do you really think so?' asked George eagerly, the tones of defeat I had detected earlier quite gone.

'I've seen rivers rise incredibly quickly after a storm and fall just as quickly,' commented Syd, drawing on his superior knowledge of the other rivers he had fished.

'What are we going to do till then?' George asked.

'You obviously missed your game of dominoes last night, and the Square and Compass is only just down the road, so why don't we have a game while we pass the time?' I suggested. George's face lit up, while Syd and Arnie, who never missed the opportunity for a pint and a friendly game, were wreathed in smiles.

George was difficult to contain. He hurried back to the car and changed with considerable speed. As soon as we released a wader, he grabbed the boot before we had completely removed it in his eagerness to pack everything into the car. 'They will have a set of dominoes, won't they?' he kept saying, even though we tried to pacify him by saying that we had never come across a public house that had not. He sped off up the track to unfasten and hold back the gate giving access to the road, even before I had fastened my shoes and started the car. He looked like a demented policeman, waving his arms frantically as he guided me out onto the road. I could not see in either direction so I had to rely on George who, after signalling me to stop while a car went past, was waving me forward with both arms and with great confidence.

'Ten minutes on point duty and you would need a rest,' said Arnie in his usual dry and phlegmatic manner.

'He's much more interesting than a set of traffic lights,' added Syd, enjoying a situation where someone other than himself was bearing the brunt of friendly ridicule.

'And just as colourful,' I said, pointing to George's face, which was flushed with the effort of running up the track and directing me safely out onto the road. George refused to be drawn by these comments, which was most unusual for him.

'He won't even mind if he draws me as a partner and we're defeated if I lose the pattern of play while I'm talking,' said Syd who, like his fishing, did not take the game too seriously or profess to be a good player.

This comment was too much for George who, by nature, always played to win. 'I will!' he barked, as if he had been stabbed in the back.

'Hello, he's back to normal,' I said to Arnie and, turning to George, 'I wish trout were like you, because I reckon the way you bite I would hook every one.'

Once settled in the Square and Compass, Arnie talked Syd into buying the first round, while George anxiously asked the landlord if he possessed a set of dominoes. He produced several sets and asked George to make his choice, then a

189

playing board with raised edges to stop the dominoes from sliding off, which he placed on our table after moving our pints to each corner. Then he hurried off, returning with a well polished mahogany score board which had bone pegs to record the points. 'If you want another drink, just give me a shout and I'll bring them across to you so that you don't have to interrupt your game,' he said before returning to his position behind the bar.

'Just listen to that,' said George as he turned the box over, letting the dominoes spill out and fall with a clatter onto the hard wooden board. He shuffled them with his head lowered to the board and turned on one side, so that his ear could savour the sound of the familiar rattle they made when they bumped against each other. 'What a beautiful sound they make,' he rapturised before ordering us to draw out for partners, which we did by taking a domino each and counting the spots: the two with the most spots and the two with the least played together.

'Oh dear, I have the honour of playing with him,' I said, referring to Syd who was already talking to the landlord and complimenting him on his friendly and efficient service. George nudged him and asked him whether he was playing or talking, adding in tones of despair that it was his drop.

'Oh, is it, me old beauty?' said Syd. 'I didn't know we had drawn for the drop.'

'We did that about ten minutes ago,' George replied impatiently, which was a slight exaggeration.

Syd and I won the first game easily. 'Well played, partner,' I said, which I knew would upset George, graciously accepting threepence from Arnie.

'Rubbish! He doesn't deserve threepence, playing like that,' spluttered George. He went through the game, pointing out Syd's errors and asking how he managed to get away with so much bad play.

'I could understand him quite easily,' I said.

'You couldn't possibly,' argued George.

190

I insisted it was quite straightforward, although this was far from the truth. When I partnered Syd I ignored all the basic rules of the game and philosophically trusted to luck and good fortune. I accepted that the subtleties would be lost on Syd and that he was not trying to convey anything to me by the way he played. Sometimes this instinctive play enabled me to win with him, but more often than not, over a long period, whoever partnered Syd would lose.

'You can't follow that kind of play,' George continued, still seething at our good fortune, and reluctantly tossed threepence across to Syd, while the ever-studious and placid Arnie remained detached from the argument, preferring to enjoy his pipe.

Nothing could bring a smile to George's face when he and Arnie lost the next game just as convincingly. 'It's like taking candy from a baby,' I said to Syd, adding fuel to a fire which was already burning well. We were well in the lead in the next game when Fred walked in.

'What's the river level like now?' Arnie asked, almost before he was through the door.

'It looks to have fallen well, and it's clearing rapidly,' Fred replied.

'Do you think we'll cast a fly onto it today?' Arnie asked, still keen to fish if there was the slightest opportunity.

'Oh, without a doubt,' Fred said optimistically.

'I hope we do better at that,' muttered George.

Syd immediately struck up a dialogue with Fred, which ruined his wavering concentration. He involved the landlord from time to time, which meant he had to turn round and look anywhere but at the board and what had been played. I slid six separate threepences across to Arnie who was casually stacking the coins at his corner of the board, reminding me of how many games we had lost. I persevered until George asked me if I could understand how Syd was playing now, and reminded me that I had not won a game for well over an hour.

'How can I win when I'm playing three of you?' I snapped at George and then asked Syd whose side he thought he was supposed to be on.

'Who's just taken a fly now?' George asked, fully recovered from his anger at losing the first two games so drastically. Arnie was still keen to fish and suggested that we go back to have a look at the water, hoping that the level had dropped and that it had cleared sufficiently to give us a few hours on the river. Syd pointed out that it was nearly closing time anyway, and a breath of fresh air would do him good. George had temporarily forgotten the river while he was winning, although I am sure it would have been mentioned some time earlier if he had continued to lose.

'I'm all for that,' I said to Arnie, pleased at the thought of being saved from yet another ignominious defeat. George replaced the dominoes in the box and gratefully handed them back to the landlord. Fred left with us and began his walk down the river while we drove back to the car park.

'The water's way down,' said Arnie, standing on the bank and knowledgeably surveying the scene. He asked me if I thought a certain tree had been in the water when we left. I told him that I was sure it had been, and agreed that the river had fallen dramatically, although it was still fairly well coloured. George and Syd walked down the river some way before they returned and made a similar assessment. I looked at Arnie and Arnie looked at me before we simultaneously asked, 'Did you see that?' in a fairly well controlled duet. We must have been watching the same small back eddy which was created by a tree. We were both convinced that we had seen a dimple. We stared, hardly daring to breathe, until we could see more rings radiating in the eddy from where a fish had taken a fly. We pointed this out to George and Syd who were still pessimistic about our prospects.

'Well, what are we going to do?' asked George, waiting by the car for orders to begin taking everything out of the boot.

'I'm all for getting changed and going fishing,' Arnie said in an unusually decisive manner.

'So am I,' I said. 'We are here now, and although the river is still up and a little cloudy, if one fish is rising there must be many more.' With that, George began to move, pleased that someone had finally made a decision.

'Where are you heading for?' I asked Arnie as soon as he was ready. He told me he was heading downstream. George informed us that he would go to the cow-drink to have a look at the marker and hoped that the river had fallen enough for him to be able to wade. Syd, with his team of wet flies, asked Arnie if he could accompany him and fish the normally shallow and streamy water, which was about halfway down the river. Syd was always fascinated by this stretch and held it in high regard, although I cannot remember him catching a single fish there.

I looked at the fish rising in the back eddy in front of the tree which was on my side of the river. I might as well have a cast at that fish, I thought, but how? This made me stop to consider the best way of approaching it. He was rising in the water which was circulating up towards the tree in the opposite direction to the main flow of the river. If the fish was facing the current he must be looking in my direction, so I must get above him. I walked out into the field, away from the river, before returning when I was well above the tree. I dropped down the steep bank at the edge of the field, to a secondary bank which led along the river almost at water level. I crouched down behind the tree and looked into the back eddy, although much of it was hidden by the trunk. I could not see the rise until I was almost up to the tree. There was the fish, rising well and completely unaware that I was watching him. He must be only a yard from me, I estimated, and I began to appreciate the possible advantages of the rather cloudy water. I could see numerous olives being dragged from the main flow to circulate temporarily in the eddy before disappearing into the fish's mouth.

How will the fly react? I wondered, looking at the river; it was flowing away from me, but the tree diverted some of the flow which was turning and heading back towards me. I worked out that although I was close to the fish, a direct cast would only allow about a second before the main flow would pull my fly line with it and drag the fly away from the fish. About three yards of slack line cast onto the water would be enough to allow the fly to complete the circulation in the back eddy, I thought.

I knelt on the bank in a position which enabled me to cast with my rod out over the water. I released some line from the reel. Two false casts were all that I needed to release the required length of line which I allowed to fall onto the river. My theories worked like a dream: the fly landed and had time to circulate in the back eddy and travel towards the fish while the fly line was straightening out in the main flow. As soon as the fly floated over where the fish was rising it disappeared. I waited, giving the fish time to turn with the fly before I lifted the rod and set the hook. Nothing much happened after that. The fish swam around for a while before I drew him towards me and lifted him out of the water with my net.

As soon as I tried to hold him to remove the hook, however, he suddenly came to life. He jumped, wriggled and thrashed about in the net, showering me with water. I tried to press him against the bank to suppress him. I even spoke to him in an educated manner and tried to reason with him, telling him that if only he had the sense to hold still for a minute I would soon have him back in the water. I sympathised with his predicament in an attempt to pacify him, telling him that I would have been annoyed to have been caught and netted like that. I resorted to chastising him. 'Don't be so silly,' I could hear myself saying. 'Why don't you stop being so stupid? You've got to tire sometime, so why bother making such a fuss?' This seemed to work because I did manage to hold him just long enough to remove the hook and move towards the water's edge, although even then he had the last word by releasing himself from my hand and jumping the final yard into the river.

How strange, I thought when the sound of the splash had faded and the turbulence of his entry had subsided. Why didn't he put up such a prolonged and energetic fight while he was in the river? It was almost as if he was not expecting to be caught in such conditions and was very surprised that he had been. Was he so confident that he was safe, so sure that no one would be fishing, that the realisation of capture did not become apparent until he was clear of the water? Or was he disorientated by the opaque water and did not know where to run?

The next fish I found was only a few yards further up the river, but rising very close to the opposite bank. I knew that, even in normal conditions, the water was deep on my side of the river, so I accepted that it would be impossible to wade. I must try to reach him, I thought, turning round to look at the bank behind me, which was almost vertical with its grassy edge way above my head. It would be a very long cast, and I must clear the bank by lifting the line over it. I made myself as secure as possible on the wet grass by the water's edge. I decided that, instead of lifting the rod to the vertical position, which would send the line horizontally back and become entangled with the bank, I would stop the rod just short. This should send the line upwards, at an angle of about thirty degrees from the top of the rod, which I considered would be just enough to clear the bank and send the back-cast out over the field.

This worked perfectly until the length of line was almost enough to reach the fish. Another yard will just about be sufficient, I thought, pulling a few more feet of line from the reel. It was. Just enough for the fly to catch the grass on the top of the bank on the forward cast, which stopped the line with a sudden jerk. I gently tried to tease it free and then tugged with more pressure, but the fly stayed obstinately and annoyingly firm. I climbed disconsolately up the slippery bank to untie a neat half-hitch and release the fly from a very unyielding piece of grass. It did not seem many minutes before I was again at the top of the bank, releasing my fly from another piece of grass which was bent where it had been strangled by the nylon.

I did not have to climb the bank when I felt and recognised the next tug. The line went tight, putting a bend and a strain on the rod, then suddenly it recoiled towards me. Yards of line catapulted from the bank, which had me instantly festooned. It was over my shoulders, around my waist and even between my legs as I turned round and round looking for ways to free it. It hung from my rod like semi-circles of spaghetti and was attached to it at the most unusual places. It managed to tie itself around each buckle on my waders and grab hold of my net and bag which were lying on the ground. In seconds I was trussed up like a festive turkey with the weight of the net and the bag tightening the line as they followed my every move. I tried to lift some line over my head, but it only went tight under one of my armpits. I could do with some advice from Houdini, I thought, straining to look down my own back to see where some of the line was attached. I began to make some progress when I removed my coat over my head as if it had been a pullover; most of the line went with it, although during this struggle I also had to wrestle with the net, which had opened out and fallen over my face like a bee-keeper's head-guard. I spent ages undoing loops, freeing my net and bag, releasing the line from my waders and clearing the coils from my rod, before all the line was back on the reel. For some time I deliberated whether it was worth having another attempt at reaching the fish. I was beginning to have problems with my conscience. Half of it was telling me to give up, while the other was scornfully asking me whether I was going to be beaten by a few blades of grass. Of course I can't give up so

196

easily, I thought, but I'll only have one more try. I looked across at the unperturbed fish.

The line began to arc out over the water and up over the bank, gradually increasing in distance as I deliberately released only small lengths of line from my reel in an attempt to keep it under control. One final effort thrust it forward. I watched intently as it flew across the river, taking the fly towards the opposite bank. 'Go on, go on!' I was urging it forward towards the rising fish, but it settled on the water some twelve agonising inches short. 'Just one more,' pleaded my conscience, and once more the fly fell tantalisingly short. I could not resist another attempt, which once again caught the grass behind me, and that, I accepted, was the end of my challenge. I had exerted all my energy in those last two casts in a supreme effort to cover the fish. My arm was tired and heavy and I could sense that it was not flexing the rod with enough power to lift the line over the bank. 'If only the rod was twelve inches longer, it would have made it so much easier,' I contemplated, going in search of another fish.

My next two quarries were far more considerate, rising only a few feet apart in a bay where the river narrowed and the bank was much less steep. The first one immediately took the fly and put up much more of a fight, although he was still not as active as I had come to expect. One theory which went through my mind as I returned him to the water was that they must have been fighting the heavy water for several hours after the storm and had lost some of their energy, although I should have thought that the heavier water would help them, and would work in their favour.

I checked to make sure that the other fish was still rising, and was pleased to see that he had not been disturbed by the commotion I had created so close to him. I was convinced that if the water had been low and clear, he would certainly have been frightened by the struggles of the first fish, which would have stopped him feeding and sent him looking for a safer place to lie for a while. I had seen this happen on many previous occasions, when fish had stopped rising after I had caught one in their vicinity. I wondered whether the alarm signal was the sight of a fish in distress, or whether the underwater sounds gave the alarm. They could certainly pick up signals from the other wildlife. Many times, while I was watching a trout, a moorhen or water vole would paddle right over where the fish was rising. At first this used to upset me, until I realised that if things took their natural course the fish would ignore the brief intrusion and continue to rise; after all, they were all creatures of the river and had to live together in some sort of harmony. I would watch a water vole heading towards a fish, hoping and praying, sometimes even subconsciously ordering it to turn away, until I learned from experience that if I kept quiet and did not disturb it, no harm would be done. If I inadvertently frightened it, the animal would scurry for safety over the rising fish and stop it feeding, which suggested to me that it had received transmitted fear.

The most amazing evidence of how discerning fish can be, and how they can apparently distinguish between the human and animal form, was once very clearly illustrated to me when some cows and I were heading for the same cow-drink. I estimated their pace and mine and equated it to the distance involved from my position on the riverside and theirs, some way out in the field, which suggested that we would arrive at more or less the same time. I began to hurry in a bid to beat them to it and head them off, but they must have recognised what I was up to because they increased their pace and proved that their four legs were far superior to my two, although I only lost the race by a short head.

'That's ruined that for me,' I said to one or two who were standing with smug looks on their faces and signs of disdain in those doleful eyes, as they awaited their turn to drink in a very ladylike and patient manner. I was fascinated watching the cows quenching their thirst by noisily sucking in gallons of water from the surface of the river. I must remember to tell Syd what he reminds me of when he takes the top off his pint, I thought, as they changed places.

Then I looked at the river. I was astonished to see fish still rising opposite the cows, and even more surprised when I saw the movement of trout feeding below them. Rather than fish elsewhere, I waited until all the cows had left because I wanted to see what effect my presence would have when I stood in the water at the cow-drink. Instead of crouching, trying to conceal my presence, I walked straight down the bank and entered the water in much the same way as the cows had done. The fish above the cow-drink, facing upstream and looking away from me, kept on rising, while those opposite and below stopped rising immediately. They could see me and were obviously afraid and alarmed by my presence. I have always been puzzled by what happened and have never managed to explain how fish can recognise and distinguish between what is safely acceptable and the threat of the hunter.

I caught the second fish and four more after that, before walking round a bend in the river to the shallows where George was fishing. On my way up, I looked at places where fish usually fed and watched the different ways the river behaved with the increase in its height. I could begin to understand why the fish had moved from these areas which were boiling and turbulent. All the fish I had seen and caught were lying in the slacker water or in the relative calm of the back eddies where the pressure was greatly reduced. There were fewer fish rising than usual, although I had more sport in those few hours than I sometimes had during a whole day. They were much less circumspect about taking the fly, which made me wonder if the water had impaired their acute vision and concealed the colour of the flies, making the artificial and the natural patterns look alike.

'How many?' I asked when I reached George, who was still industriously working a fly over the shallows. Before he could answer he struck and was playing a fish which seemed far more active than those I had caught. I could not help smiling when the fish darted towards George and leaped out of the water on its way past, just as if it was waving goodbye. 'Where are you going?' I could hear George asking. 'Come back!' he called as he stumbled round through one hundred and eighty degrees to face the fish, which was by now well downstream. He managed to talk the fish back towards him by telling himself to be careful and the fish to come on. 'That's five,' he said, holding a very nice grayling high above the water in his net. He continued talking to himself on his way out of the river, and pretended to make the task look more precarious than it really was, no doubt to enhance his achievements. I, meanwhile, was delighted with his success.

I do not know why, but George and Arnie always caught fewer fish than I did, with George usually catching the least. They accepted that if I was catching fish they stood a chance. They would ask how many I had caught when I met them at lunchtime, and if I told them I had only caught one they would become discouraged, saying that they had no hope of success. Fred began to ask me how I was catching fish and what fly I was using, which was quite the reverse of what happened when I first began fishing. One day I overheard him talking to the water bailiff. They were discussing the difficulties of catching fish on the Derwent when he said, 'If he can't catch any here, then no one will.' I felt very proud and honoured when I realised that Fred was referring to me.

As soon as George reached the bank, I went down to hold his rod, so that he could deal with the fish. I asked him where he had caught the others. He told me he had not moved from the spot where I had found him and that as soon as he had caught one fish others began to rise. He was like a dog with two tails, describing the difficulties he had encountered with each fish — the way they had fought and how he had nearly lost his balance in the river.

'That's five in a few hours,' I said. 'That's more than you've ever caught in a day.'

'I know, it's ridiculous,' he laughed. 'I'm glad we stayed after all.'

'What's ridiculous?' I asked.

'Oh,' he said, 'if we had known what the river looked like first thing this morning we wouldn't even have left home. What a day! Five in a few hours. By the way, how many have you caught?'

'Five,' I said quickly. I could not spoil his pleasure by telling him that I had caught seven, so I let two of the fish slip from my memory, sink and slowly swim away in the murky waters.

'Come on, let's go and see how Syd and Arnie have done,' I said. George could not believe that it was almost time to leave and wondered how he could have spent so much time in one place. I explained that it was quite easy. We had just arrived at the place where I had tried to reach the other bank.

'Just look there,' I said. 'That well-trodden grass is where I spent ages casting to that fish,' and I pointed across to where he was still rising, quite unconcerned. George asked me if I had managed to cast close to him and I told him the story, while I stood at the top of the bank looking down at the battered grass. A pair of shears, I suggested, would have been a welcome piece of equipment.

Arnie was also pleased with his fishing, and so was Syd who had caught two from the streamy water he favoured so much.

'Just ask George how many he's had,' I said, looking at George who was still smiling contentedly.

'Come on then, how many?' asked Syd.

'Five,' he muttered, 'a great day,' becoming slightly embarrassed at being the centre of attention.

Once he had walked round the car two or three times to make sure nothing was left, he ambled up the track to open the gate. How strange, I thought. Only a few hours ago he was rushing about as if there was no tomorrow, and now he's taking his time and totally relaxed. He even made himself comfortable by leaning on the wall on the opposite side of the road while he calmly waited for a gap in the traffic so that he could signal me out.

When we had settled round one of the tables in the Chequers, I asked George and Arnie what fly patterns they had been using. George had used his faithful Kite's Imperial, while Arnie had caught all his fish on a Greenwell's Glory. I had caught mine on a Grey Duster.

'I thought so,' I said. 'We all caught fish on different patterns, in both shape and colour. Those fish would have taken anything within reason today.'

'I'm sure they would,' agreed Arnie. 'And another thing that struck me today was how wrong the books can be. They always suggest that fish won't rise in a swollen and coloured river. I know we haven't seen so many fish, but we have had one of those days on the river when we just could not fail.'

'I hope we have another storm and a coloured river before the end of the season if the fishing is so good,' George said, looking forward to another successful day.

'Don't mention the end of the season,' Arnie pleaded, not wishing to be reminded of the inevitable, which was quickly creeping up on us.

* * *

We approached the end of our first full season with mixed feelings and differing views. It was always pleasant when Saturday arrived, although once September began we realised that each one would take us closer to the end of the season. George and Syd did not seem to mind too much, judging from their comments about how much they were looking forward to the grayling fishing throughout the winter months. Syd I could understand: he fished his fly patterns under the water and, although I realise it is a completely different technique using different tackle, to replace the wet fly with a maggot was not in essence so very different. He liked his chat and company, so he would not mind sitting within talking distance and holding a conversation while he fished. George made me wonder. He had persevered with the fly and had now caught numerous fish, which I thought would have changed his attitude. He looked forward to every Saturday and would spend as long as he could on the bank, casting a fly. I could not understand how, after all that he had learned and the success he had achieved with the fly, he could so easily revert to watching a float trot down the river, or how he could suggest that this held the same fascination and sense of satisfaction as fly fishing.

Arnie and I were dedicated to the fly and would have fished it all the time if that were possible. Arnie was dreading the end of the season when the fly would become only a memory and the river would be comparatively lifeless, devoid of rising fish. He was a true fisherman and would fish through the winter months for grayling, but I knew that, while he sat on his box, he would be thinking about casting a fly and looking forward to the first signs of spring. I felt much the same, although the end of the season had a charm of its own. I loved the cool September mornings, when the mist lay in horizontal strands in the valleys and the sun illuminated the tops of the hills. I looked for the first tree to show signs of autumn and watched the bracken begin to shrink and lose some of its life. The river seemed to wake up a little later, after the chill of the night. The trees appeared to be crying, shedding drops of heavy dew into the water from leaves which would soon be changing their colour and succumbing to the first frost and the wind.

I was not looking forward to the next few months after the end of the season; March would seem an age away, although at least we would have some fishing and a reason for being out in the fresh air. But my attitude to the long, dark winter nights changed when, just before the end of the season, I went to Tom Saville's Tackle Shop. The shop was only six miles from home, which was far more convenient than making the long journey to Ashbourne. I had come to know Ken Smith, the manager, quite well because the amount of fishing I did and the way I kept losing flies made frequent visits necessary. As well as catering for fishermen, the shop stocked all sorts of pets. Along with the more common rabbits and gerbils there were snakes, turtles, terrapins, mina birds and parrots, but the most beautiful of all the creatures on display were tank after tank of tropical fish, each one illuminated by its own light that showed off their iridescent colours to great advantage.

'What do you want today?' asked Ken, who always chose to serve any fisherman, leaving the other assistants to look after the animals, millet, budgie seed, flea powder for dogs and other pet people's sundries.

'One or two Grey Dusters,' I said, and he went to a cabinet and slid out one of the shelves. There were two cabinets in the shop, each one holding about ten trays. The shallow trays were partitioned and held about twelve lines of boxes, each one containing a different pattern of fly. What a lovely sight, I thought, looking at the extended tray with its multi-coloured flies in many different sizes, and trying to work out how many patterns there were.

'Ten lines, twelve boxes in each line, ten trays in each cabinet — you must have hundreds of patterns here,' I said to Ken as he counted out half a dozen Grey Dusters.

'Thousands,' he said. 'Mind you, many of them are designed to catch fishermen, not fish.' He chuckled.

'They must take some tying. Who ties them?' I asked.

'I do some, and we have a number of people who tie for us. Why, would you like to learn?'

I was quite taken aback by this. 'Why? How?' I questioned.

'Twelve weeks over the winter, starting in a month's time,' he replied. 'I have one place left in my Fly Tying School, so if you'd like to join us you would be most welcome.'

Suddenly, quite by chance, I could not wait for the darker

evenings. How, I wondered, could all the feathers and fur be tied onto such a small hook? How on earth did one begin?

The season ended and my first lesson was only a week away. I was impatiently looking forward to learning how to tie my own flies and perhaps master a new technique which would add another dimension, giving me a new experience to add to my knowledge of fly fishing. The evening finally arrived. It was the opening of another absorbing chapter in my life as a game fisherman and the beginning of another story.